Antiquitez de Rome

Produced in association with

Runnymede Books
Royal Holloway and Bedford New College
Egham, Surrey TW20 0EX
United Kingdom

Joachim du Bellay

Antiquitez de Rome

translated by
Edmund Spenser
as
Ruines of Rome

with notes by
Malcolm C. Smith

meɒieʋɑl & ʀenɑissɑnce texts & stuɒies
Center for Medieval & Early Renaissance Studies
Binghamton, New York
1994

ISBN 0–86698–126–8

Book design and typesetting by Philip Taylor, Royal Holloway and Bedford New College, University of London. TEXset in Adobe Palatino 9/10.8 & 10/12 pt, and processed on the Linotronic 300 of the University of London Computer Centre.

The woodcuts on pages 124–137 are reproduced by permission of *The Huntington Library, San Marino, California*; they are taken from J. van der Noot's *A theatre for worldlings*, published in 1569 (call number RB 62764).

Contents

Introduction

———◆◆◆———

The task of anyone who presents poems to an audience (as Montaigne said, in his wonderful essay *On the younger Cato*) is to speak with the voice of the poet himself, to convey the very qualities inherent in the poetry. So let me avow my ineptitude to present to you Joachim Du Bellay's *Antiquitez de Rome* and *Songe*. Has anyone ever discerned the full wealth of reflection (moral, political and especially theological) in these poems — let alone conveyed those riches to others? Has anyone ever emulated the subtlety of Du Bellay, his inspired allusiveness, his fleeting wit? The texts of his *Antiquitez de Rome* and his *Songe* must therefore be their own introduction, and you would be well advised to skip the musings in the next few pages.

In these hauntingly evocative poems, Du Bellay constantly draws the reader into a dialogue with him. For, like all the great writers of the French Renaissance, he requires a response from his reader: he offers a wealth of reflections of his own, but his aim above all is to stimulate, to provoke, to move... He appeals to your imagination, to your historical vision, to your sense of justice, to your openness to mystery. Above all, perhaps, he appeals to your humanity. For, just as he was moved to write by an intimate kinship with the ancient Romans, he invites his readers to develop a kinship with him. His readers are his unseen friends, his guests (as he put it in another of his collections, the *Regrets*) at the poetic feast he has laid out. And his audience is eternal — like-minded spirits of any epoch who can share a vision which is itself timeless.

The *Antiquitez de Rome* and *Songe* were published in the same volume in 1558. Some of Du Bellay's earlier work anticipates these poems — for example his famous prose work, the *Deffence et illustration de la langue françoyse*. In 1549, Du Bellay (who was born in 1522) had gained sudden notoriety with this work, a witty and iconoclastic diatribe against the cultural establishment and, more audaciously, against the theological establishment, the 'venerable Druids' of the Sorbonne who oppress scholars (the *Deffence* is now usually presented, ponderously and unhistorically, as a work on philology). The

Deffence foreshadows the *Antiquitez* in its self-confidence, its incisiveness, its challenges to the reader's judgement and imagination. In particular, the *Deffence* advances a claim that France can aspire to cultural supremacy over all other nations; that patriotic sentiment is found in the *Antiquitez*, a collection dedicated to the King, which hints that the future status of France will rival that of the ancient Romans.

Also in 1549, Du Bellay had published the first French collection of sonnets, *L'Olive*. As often with Du Bellay's works, there is more to these poems than meets the eye. They can be read, on a literal level, as a love story. But they also have a political dimension and a theological dimension — and in each respect, they anticipate the *Antiquitez*. The political dimension lies in the fact that his ostensible heroine, Olive, represents the sister of the King, Marguerite de France; for not only is the collection dedicated to her, but the olive was the emblem of Minerva and Marguerite was known as the 'Minerva of the Court', and was portrayed as such in royal festivities (and Du Bellay compared her to Minerva, and extolled her in many of his works). Du Bellay makes it clear in the first sonnet that in extolling her, he aims to endow the nation with a literary monument to rival those of the Italians, inventors of the sonnet. The *Antiquitez*, likewise (as we have seen) are dedicated to the King, and they contain several intimations that Du Bellay sees himself as an emulator of Latin poets.

The theological dimension in the *Olive* is seen in the fact that Du Bellay's love story starts on Christmas Day (see s. 5) and ends on Good Friday (s. 111), and the olive (as he recalls in s. 49) is a biblical symbol of reconciliation between God and man: on the theological level, Olive represents the Redeemer, and the sonnets implicitly depict mystic love as well as human love. This fact, incidentally, was lost on the illustrious Reformer Théodore de Bèze who in 1550, in the preface to his edifying play *Abraham sacrifiant*, declared that the author ought rather to write religious verse than 'petrarchise a sonnet and act as a lover in a trance' — a comment which stung Du Bellay and probably strengthened his antipathy towards the Reformation. After *L'Olive*, Du Bellay consolidated his standing as a theological poet in 1552 by publishing his miniature biblical epic, the *Monomachie de David et de Goliath*, together with other religious poems (they appeared with his verse translation of Book 4 of the *Aeneid*). It is hardly surprising, after these meditative works, to find Du Bellay presenting in the *Antiquitez* and the *Songe* an abundance of reflection on divine intervention in human affairs.

The *Antiquitez* and the *Songe* were published on Du Bellay's return from a four-year stay in Rome (1553–1557). He brought back with him three other collections of poems, all of them also published in 1558. One is a miscellany, the *Divers jeux rustiques et autres œuvres poëtiques*, which has little in common with the *Antiquitez*: the 'rustic games' of the title are translations of the *Lusus* of Andrea Navagero, and the book also contains love poetry, facetious epitaphs, satire and parody. Another of the collections written in Rome is more relevant to the *Antiquitez*: the volume titled *Poematum libri quatuor* includes the elegy *Romæ descriptio*, which contains reflections on the ruins of Rome comparable to those in the *Antiquitez*, reminding us that there are many close links between Du Bellay's Latin output and his French verse. This volume contains the Latin elegies, epigrams, love poems and epitaphs which made Du Bellay almost as famous in his own day for Latin poetry as for his French work.

The other collection published in 1558 is *Les Regrets*, a collection of elegiac and satirical sonnets based on emulation of Ovid and Horace respectively, but with much personal material derived from Du Bellay's experiences in Rome as secretary to his father's cousin, Cardinal Jean Du Bellay. These poems complement the *Antiquitez* in many ways. Both collections are in sonnet form, both are set in Rome, both present Rome as a universal symbol of mankind, both have much moral content. And the moral content is similar in each collection: the *Regrets* present the mortality of the powerful, notably the popes; the *Antiquitez* present the ruins of the Empire. Both collections are full of nostalgia and poignancy: in the *Regrets* Du Bellay, who sees himself as an exile in Rome, pines for his absent friends; in the *Antiquitez*, he laments the dead Romans. Both collections have a strong visual dimension, for Du Bellay was of the view that poetry was akin to painting. Above all, perhaps, both reveal the introspective yet affable personality of the poet. Yet the differences are equally profound: for example, in the *Regrets*, Du Bellay renounces all claim to be an inspired poet and to enjoy immortality, whereas in the *Antiquitez* he projects himself as an equal of those ancient poets who conferred such status on Rome and whose memory he so eloquently revives.

The appeal of Rome to Du Bellay, in the *Antiquitez* as well as in the *Regrets*, is as a symbol of mankind. The Rome of the *Antiquitez* is co-extensive with the world, in space (for Rome conquered the world: see sonnet 4, for example) and in time (for the authority of Rome endures still: see s. 18). Rome is thus the archetypal state. Rome is also a macrocosm: its destiny offers a model — and a warning — to anyone who reflects on that destiny. For Du Bellay applies to the city of Rome language which could as well apply to an individual, for example in s. 4, 5 and 12; and he observes in s. 23 that the state and the individual have parallel destinies. Indeed, his central reflection is that the fall of Rome came about through a vice which can affect an individual as well as a nation: pride. And the fate of Rome, like that of the individual, was to be reduced to *cendre* ('Remember, man, that thou are dust...'), and to lie in a *tombeau*...

The moral theme, that pride leads to a fall, is projected with stark clarity through antithesis. The full title of the book is antithetical: the book presents a *description generale de sa* [Rome's] *grandeur, et comme une deploration de sa ruine*. The collection itself is antithetical: words like *orgueil* are constantly contrasted with *ruine*. Very commonly, individual sonnets project this antithesis, with Du Bellay conveying the grandeur of Rome in his quatrains and its decline in the tercets. Indeed, antithesis is commonly found in individual phrases (for example, s. 3, ll. 13–14; s. 15, ll. 3–4). And the contrast between pride and fall becomes utterly dominant in the companion-piece to the *Antiquitez*, which is the curious dream-sequence, the *Songe*.

The *Songe* was very closely linked in Du Bellay's mind with the *Antiquitez*: he named the two works jointly on his titlepage, declaring that the *Songe* is 'on the same subject' as the *Antiquitez* (Spenser was to separate the two collections). The meaning of the enigmatic *Songe* has exercised many scholars (see the studies listed in the bibliography at the end of this volume). My own suggestion is as follows: in the *Antiquitez*, Du Bellay had indicated repeatedly (though, often, subtly) that the universal political jurisdiction of the state of Rome had been replaced by the universal authority of the Church of Rome; in the *Songe*, he tells us allusively that the Roman Church has been corrupted by wealth and worldliness and, when challenged by the Reformers, has followed the ancient Romans into precipitate ruin; but, unlike the Roman state, the Church is of divine foundation and will flourish anew when purged of corruption. This interpretation (the basis for it is expounded in the notes to these sonnets) is consistent with what we know of Du Bellay's religious views: appalled by the vices he witnessed at the papal court, and which he graphically portrayed in the *Regrets*, he remained committed to the Catholic faith (see the note to s. 2 of the *Antiquitez*).

Translations in blank verse of eleven of the fifteen sonnets of the *Songe* appeared in *A Theatre for worldlings* published in 1569 by Jan van der Noot. Since it is to Van der Noot that we owe the introduction of Du Bellay to an anglophone audience, and (as we shall see) the first publication of work by Spenser, it is worth pausing to recall the salient moments of his life. He had been born c. 1535 near Antwerp of a very wealthy family; he claimed descent from a Roman aristocrat and the daughter of a noble family of Brabant, whose marriage had been celebrated in the year 563! As well as Latin and some Greek, he had a near-native knowledge of French, and some Italian and Spanish. He was a deputy mayor in Antwerp in 1562 and again in 1565, and was a patron of writers as well as being a writer himself. But his prosperity came to an abrupt end: with the failure of an attempt by the Calvinists to seize power in Antwerp, he fled to London at the end of March 1567, 'as well for that I would not beholde the abhominations of the Romishe Antechrist, as to escape the handes of the bloudthirsty' (as he says in the letter which dedicates his *Theatre* to Queen Elizabeth, A iii^{ro}). He then moved to the Rhineland (in 1569) and to France (1578), where he apparently met Ronsard and Jean Dorat. He eventually felt it safe to return to Antwerp, perhaps because his religious views had evolved in the direction of Nicodemism — the belief that just as it was permissible for the disciple Nicodemus to see Christ furtively, at night, for fear of persecution, so it is permissible to conform outwardly to a prevailing (though erroneous) orthodoxy, while confessing the truth in the secrecy of one's conscience. Van der Noot was now dependent on patronage rather than a dispenser of it, and was to die in poverty and obscurity some time between 1595 and 1601. (For more information on his life, see especially the study by Brachin.)

It was in England that Van der Noot published his *Theatre*, first in a Dutch edition (dedicated on 18 September 1568 to a Dutch emigré, Sir Roger Martin or Martens, Lord Mayor of London), then in a French edition dedicated to Queen Elizabeth, dated 28 October 1568; an English translation appeared in the following year, again with a dedication to Queen Elizabeth (dated 25 May 1569); it was also to be issued in Cologne in 1572, in a German translation by Balthasar Froe. There are three main components to this *Theatre*: (i) six 'epigrams' (two of fourteen lines, the rest of twelve lines) dealing with the collapse of worldly prosperity, with a four-line 'envoy' (these epigrams are translations of poems by Clément Marot, which are themselves based on imitation of a *Canzone* by Petrarch — *Rime sparsi*, 323); (ii) a group of fifteen sonnets, the first eleven of which are translations of sonnets in the *Songe* (1–5, 7, 9–12 and 15), and the last four, apparently by Van der Noot himself, are based on passages in the book of *Revelation*; and (iii) a long religious reflection in prose which forms the main body of the work and which incorporates commentaries on the poems which preceded it.

The English translations of the poems are not credited to Spenser in the 1569 publication (a certain Theodore Roest is credited with translating the prose part of the text; for the very little that is known about Roest, see Forster in *English Studies*, 1967). The reason the poetic translations can safely be ascribed to Spenser is that the translations of Du Bellay and of Petrarch reappeared in substantially the same form in Spenser's *Complaints* of 1591 as *The Visions of Bellay* and *The Visions of Petrarch, formerly translated*; it is reasonable to surmise that Spenser had also been the author of the 1569 translation of the four sonnets by Van der Noot himself. It has been argued, in my view inconclusively, that the verse translations from the French show the influence of a Dutch version (see Pienaar and Forster, in *English Studies*, 1926 and 1967 respectively).

How did Van der Noot and Spenser come to know the work of Du Bellay? Spenser had been a pupil at the recently-founded Merchant Taylors' School, and the principal, Richard Mulcaster, appears to have been a reader of Du Bellay's *Deffence et illustration de la langue françoyse*, and to have shared Du Bellay's views on the need to enrich the vernacular tongues (see Ferguson, 'Du Bellay', in *The Spenser Encyclopedia*). Mulcaster also associated with Dutch emigrés in London, a community of affluent and erudite merchants — and Van der Noot was a member of this community. Mulcaster was also an acquaintance of Charles Uytenhove, and Uytenhove had been a close friend of Du Bellay — and a collaborator: he appears to have provided the impetus for Du Bellay's *Xenia*, a collection of poems consisting in puns on the names of illustrious contemporaries (on these connections, see the article by Galland).

Van der Noot used Du Bellay's sonnets to help project his own moral condemnation of ancient Rome. In his commentary on the eleven sonnets, Van der Noot notes that Du Bellay shows 'that all things here upon earthe are nothing but wretched miserie and miserable vanitie', and that 'Rome hath bene destroyed, which of a base and low estate was lifted up, and became very hie, and that by none other means than covetousnesse and the great desire which that people and nation had to money and ambition' (F 5^{ro-vo}); but Rome's lust for power led to divine retribution, so that the Romans 'have been justly plagued, receyving according to their desertes such measure as they have measured to others' (F 6vo). The ruins 'beare witnesse of Gods vengeance which came upon them for their sin and wickednesse, to the end that all godly and well disposed persons mighte perceive, that God can and will perfourme his promises, the which he hath thretned in his worde' (F 7ro). Du Bellay's presentation of Rome is a little more sympathetic than that, but he would hardly have dissented from those general sentiments; his sonnets do indeed depict the fate of 'worldlings'.

But Van der Noot also used Du Bellay to project his view of the papacy, as is also clear from his prose commentary on the sonnets. Du Bellay would certainly not have agreed with him that the bishops of Rome 'have banished and abolished Christe and his doctrine' (G i^{ro-vo}) and that 'their doctrine and teaching is nothing but death and damnation' (G ii^{ro}). The *Theatre for worldlings* is largely a deprecation of papal Rome — scholars have discerned in it the influence of the Reformed theologians John Bale and Heinrich Bullinger (on this aspect of the work, see the article by Rasmussen). Du Bellay was certainly an acerbic commentator on corruption in the papal court: his four years in the household of an influential cardinal gave him an unrivalled insider's view of the decadence — which, as we have seen, he depicted in the *Regrets*. But Du Bellay distinguished between the personal lives of the popes and the authority of the papacy, and there are indications of this even in the *Songe*. The reason Van der Noot was able to harness most of the *Songe* to the anti-papal cause is that the sonnets are enigmatic and allusive.

Besides offering a commentary on the sonnets, Van der Noot has another way of ensuring that Du Bellay's work is projected in an anti-papal manner. The *Songe* contained fifteen sonnets. Van der Noot omitted four of them (6, 8, 13 and 14), and at least one of these, s. 13, appears to defend papal doctrine and to allude disparagingly to the Reformation (see the note in this edition). To make the number of sonnets up to the original fifteen, Van der Noot added four of his own which draw on passages of the *Apocalypse* commonly used by Reformers to denounce the Church of Rome. Thus, s. 12, the first by Van der Noot, is a paraphrase of *Apocalypse* XIII and shows the dragon (who, in the *Apocalypse*, represents Satan) handing over power to the seven-headed beast (Rome); one of the beast's heads has recently been wounded (by the gospel, Van der Noot explains in his prose commentary). The next sonnet, again derived from the *Apocalypse* (chapters XVII–XVIII), shows the whore of Babylon (here representing the Roman Church) sitting on the beast and drinking the blood of martyrs, until an angel declares that Babylon is fallen. Sonnet 14, derived from *Apocalypse* XIX, shows the destruction of the beast and the pagan kings; and sonnet 15 depicts the heavenly Jerusalem of *Apocalypse* XXI–XXII. Du Bellay's *Songe* is thus pressed into the service of the Reformation; the poet would certainly have disowned this use of his work. Van der Noot's four sonnets are reproduced in this edition along with the 1569 translation of the eleven sonnets from the *Songe*, so you can see something of the context in which Du Bellay's work first appeared in English.

In one interesting way, however, Van der Noot is faithful to the spirit of Du Bellay. The Frenchman's poems appeal to the reader's imagination and conjure up pictures: they are highly visual. Indeed, Du Bellay repeatedly compared his poetry to painting (and, in so doing, was following in a very long tradition: see my note to the dedicatory poem in the *Antiquitez*). It was thus highly appropriate that Van der Noot accompanied the texts of Du Bellay (or, in the English version, the translations) with illustrations. The result is that the *Theatre* resembles the then highly-popular emblem books, in which epigrams with moral significance were accompanied by elucidatory pictures. The designer of the fourteen woodcuts in the English edition of the *Theatre*, which are reproduced here, may have been Marcus Gheeraerts the Elder, another refugee in London (he is also the probable author of the copperplates which illustrate the Dutch and English editions of the *Theatre*; see the article by Bath, p. 82).

For his 1591 *Complaints*, Spenser polished his 1569 version of the *Songe*. His sonnets are now in rhyme rather than (as in 1569) in blank verse; and the 1591 translation is complete — he added translations of the four sonnets from the *Songe* which been missing in the *Theatre* of 1569. Also (and most importantly), Spenser included in the 1591 publication his translation of Du Bellay's *Antiquitez*; so far as is known, the translation had not appeared before. Although his translations of the two collections by Du Bellay appeared in the same volume, Spenser did not otherwise link them, even though Du Bellay had done so in his title, which specifies that they are both on the same subject. Spenser also omitted the subtitle which Du Bellay gave the *Antiquitez*: the subtitle is an important guide to the nature of the collection, since it points to the antithetical presentation of the material (on the grandeur and the ruin of Rome).

But Spenser's most interesting alterations are in the translations of the sonnets themselves. Of course, translation in the Renaissance (and especially translation of poetry) was regarded as a creative process analogous to that which had produced the original work; translators were not expected to be as literally faithful as would now be the case. I have not listed every minor departure from Du Bellay — some were doubtless influenced by exigencies of rhyme or metre — but, at the risk of appearing anachronistic, I have pointed to Spenser's principal departures from the original, and have done so for three main reasons. One is simply to add to the usefulness of Spenser's translation as an aid to the understanding of the original texts; Spenser will give a great deal of help with the French to those who need it, but he is not a wholly reliable guide. Another is to help make it possible to determine how much French Spenser knew: if we can settle that question, we shall be better able to distinguish between those departures from Du Bellay which are inadvertent and those which are deliberate — a distinction which needs to be made if we are to use these poems as a basis for judgements on Spenser's aesthetics or his opinions. And the third reason for pointing to Spenser's departures from the French is their historical interest; most notably, he filtered out the Roman Catholic sentiment found in Du Bellay's texts (see especially the note to the translation of *Antiquitez*, s. 17). Curiously, most of these alterations seem to have escaped the attention of modern writers on Spenser.

Du Bellay appears to have provided an important stimulus to Spenser's subsequent career as a poet (see Ferguson, 'Du Bellay', in *The Spenser Encyclopedia*). Indeed, his *Antiquitez de Rome* stimulated a very great number of other poets: without looking very hard, I have found no fewer than twenty-eight poems written in the sixteenth and seventeenth centuries, in eight languages, which echo just one of Du Bellay's sonnets (or its model: see the note to s. 3 of the *Antiquitez*); and Kent Hieatt has pointed to echoes of Spenser's translation of Du Bellay in Shakespeare's *Sonnets*. The *fortuna* of Du Bellay's poems and of Spenser's translation has yet to be adequately studied. It is my hope that the present publication will assist scholars who want to investigate this and other issues. But my greater hope is that this edition will bring these poems to a wider audience than has enjoyed them hitherto. Du Bellay's poems are inspired; Spenser's translations are readable, have literary and historical interest, and will, for many, help make Du Bellay's text accessible.

This is the first time Du Bellay's sonnets and Spenser's translations have been published in the same volume. The texts presented in this edition are based on copies of the original editions in the British Library:

Le premier livre des Antiquitez de Rome, contenant une generale description de sa grandeur, et comme une deploration de sa ruine: par Joach[im] *Dubellay Ang*[evin]. *Plus un Songe ou vision sur le mesme subject, du mesme autheur,* A Paris, de l'imprimerie de Federic Morel, rue S. Jan de Beauvais, au franc Meurier, M.D.LVIII, Avec privilege du Roy (839 h 22 (2));

Complaints. Containing sundrie small Poemes of the Worlds Vanitie. Whereof the next Page maketh mention. By Ed[mund] *Sp*[enser]. London. Imprinted for William Ponsonbie, dwelling in Paules Churchyard at the signe of the Bishops Head, 1591 (C 39 e 5 (2)); and

A Theatre wherein be represented as wel the miseries & calamities that follow the voluptuous Worldlings, as also the greate joyes and plesures which the faithfull do enjoy. An argument both profitable and delectable, to all that sincerely love the word of God. Devised by S. John vander Noodt. Seene and allowed according to the order appointed. Imprinted at London by Henry Bynneman. Anno Domini 1569 (224 a 11).

In accordance with usual scholarly practice in editing French sixteenth-century texts, I have retained the original spelling except where it is necessary to add accents to differentiate between words (*ou* and *où*, etc.), but have adopted modern conventions in punctuation; and I have applied these principles to the translations as well as the original text.

The bibliography lists what I regard as the best editions of Du Bellay and a selection of the most important historical and critical studies.

Malcolm C Smith
London, September 1993

Antiquitez de Rome (1558)

Ruines of Rome (1591)

A poem written for Henry II, who died grievously in jousting 2 years later.

Refers to renaissance, but not directly. Just hints at it by the 'dissinterman and 'rebuilding.

~ *Au Roy* ~

stones

Ne vous pouvant donner ces ouvrages antiques
  Pour vostre Sainct-Germain ou pour Fontainebleau,
Je les vous donne (Sire) en ce petit tableau
Peint, le mieux que j'ay peu, de couleurs poëtiques :
    Qui, mis sous vostre nom devant les yeux publiques,
Si vous le daignez voir en son jour le plus beau,
Se pourra bien vanter d'avoir hors du tumbeau
Tiré des vieux Romains les poudreuses reliques.
    Que vous puissent les Dieux un jour donner tant d'heur
De rebastir en France une telle grandeur
Que je la voudrois bien peindre en vostre langage :
    Et peult estre qu'alors vostre grand' majesté,
Repensant à mes vers, diroit qu'ilz ont esté
De vostre Monarchie un bienheureux presage.

Pragmatic sonnet:
① Poetry is a picture
② dissinterment.
③ Rebuilding

Where abbreviated bibliographical information is given, please see the Bibliography.

Au Roy. The *Antiquitez* (Du Bellay declares) are patriotic poems: in bringing back to life the ancient Romans, he prefigures that universal dominion (*Monarchie*, l. 14) which France will enjoy. Henry II of France had imperial ambitions — enshrined in his emblem, the crescent moon and the motto *Donec totum impleat orbem* ('Until he fill the whole orb'; on Henry's ambition and the origin of his device, see Hartley, *Patriotism in Du Bellay*, p. 57 and notes). Du Bellay adds that when Henry has conquered the world, he (the poet) will extol his achievement. He saw the writing of patriotic poetry as being the classic role of a poet (see lines 9–11 and *Deffence et illustration*, pp. 184–185; *Œuvres poëtiques*, III, pp. 72–74; VI, p. 53); and in this, he drew on a vibrant Roman tradition (see Hartley, pp. 13–20 and notes).

The comparison between poetry and painting (ll. 1–4, 11) is very ancient. 'Painting is a silent poem and poetry is a talking picture', wrote Simonides of Ceos (and see Horace's *Ars poetica*, l. 361; Plutarch, *Moralia*, ed. F.C. Babbitt, I, pp. 90–93; Quainton, 'Morte peinture [. . .]'). Du Bellay's use of the analogy is highly apposite to the *Antiquitez*. The comparison recurs later (s. 5, 25) and is used elsewhere by Du Bellay (*Les Regrets*, s. 1, 21, 62, 148; *Deffence et illustration*, p. 7, 38, 41, 43, 147, 182; *Olive*, pp. 50–51; *Divers jeux rustiques*, p. 69; *Œuvres poëtiques*, VI, pp. 164–165).

Edmund Spenser, doubtless disinclined to extol a French monarch, omitted this poem from his translation of the *Antiquitez*.

(handwritten top:) 'A ray' → Buildings being disinterred/ressurection.
'1st sonnet' → people " — " " — "

(handwritten:) Both positive and ambiguous value.
very dense poetry → each word seems to have a particular connotation.

20

~ 1 ~

(handwritten left:) covered up with so many walls.

(handwritten above line:) Divine spirits   powdery ashes → compares to powdery remains in "Au Roy."

Divins Esprits, dont la poudreuse cendre
Gist sous le faix de tant de murs couvers,
Non vostre loz, qui vif par voz beaux vers
Ne se verra sous la terre descendre :

(handwritten left:) He's saying that their importance as poets, their glory and praise will never die. Just as poetic immortality won't ever die.

Si des humains la voix se peult estendre
Depuis icy jusqu'au fond des enfers,
Soient à mon cry les abysmes ouvers,
Tant que d'abas vous me puissiez entendre.

(handwritten right:) If my race can be heard from here, on earth where I stand, to the bottom of hell, then let the earth open up, So you in the underworld can hear me.

(handwritten left:) He claims he'll go round the divine spirits' tombs 3 times, calling out 3 times

(handwritten:) numéro magique

Trois fois cernant sous le voile des cieux
De voz tumbeaux le tour devotieux,
A haulte voix trois fois je vous appelle :
J'invoque icy vostre antique fureur,
En ce pendant que d'une saincte horreur
Je vays chantant vostre gloire plus belle.

(handwritten:) Carmen → Poet ∴ poet is magician with words
chârme → spell

(handwritten bottom left:) He's undertaking a magical ritual

Sonnet 1. The *Divins Esprits* are those of the ancient Roman poets, and Du Bellay invokes their *antique fureur* (poetic inspiration). Echoing their classical ancestors, Renaissance poets frequently stressed the need for inspiration (see especially the famous ode of 1552 which Ronsard dedicated to Michel de L'Hospital). In this sonnet, Du Bellay hints that if he enjoys the same inspiration as the ancient Romans, he will share their immortality. He claims immortality for his collection again in s. 25 and 32.

   This sonnet has a tone of religious awe. The poet three times walks round the ancient poets' tombs, and three times invokes them: on the use of this number in religious rites, see Saulnier, p. 115. The sonnet contrasts with the opening sonnets of the *Regrets*, where Du Bellay says he lacks inspiration and can no longer aspire to immortal fame: the various contrasts between the two collections heighten the specific qualities of each.

~ 1 ~

Ye heavenly spirites, whose ashie cinders lie
  Under deep ruines, with huge walls opprest,
But not your praise, the which shall never die
Through your faire verses, ne in ashes rest:
  If so be shrilling voyce of wight alive
May reach from hence to depth of darkest hell,
Then let those deep Abysses open rive,
That ye may understand my shreiking yell.
  Thrice having seene under the heavens veale
Your toombs devoted compasse over all,
Thrice unto you with lowd voyce I appeale,
And for your antique furie here doo call,
  The whiles that I with sacred horror sing
  Your glorie, fairest of all earthly thing.

————◆◆◆————

The translation. 'Rive' (l. 7): 'to cleave', 'split asunder'. There is nothing in the original which corresponds directly to Spenser's 'shrilling' (l. 5) and 'shreiking' (l. 8); and 'fairest of all earthly thing' (l. 14) is an elaboration. Spenser seems to have misunderstood lines 9–10, which describe a ritual: Du Bellay walks devoutly round the tombs of the ancient poets three times (*cerner* means 'To incircle, compasse with a circle; inviron, or inclose round about; also, to make a round, fetch a compasse, wheele about' (Randle Cotgrave, *A dictionarie of the French and English tongues*, London, 1611).

~ 2 ~

Le Babylonien ses haults murs vantera
Et ses vergers en l'air, de son Ephesienne
La Grece descrira la fabrique ancienne,
Et le peuple du Nil ses pointes chantera ;
 La mesme Grece encor vanteuse publira
De son grand Juppiter l'image Olympienne,
Le Mausole sera la gloire Carienne,
Et son vieux Labyrinth' la Crete n'oublira ;
 L'antique Rhodien elevera la gloire
De son fameux Colosse au temple de Memoire,
Et si quelque œuvre encor digne se peult vanter
 De marcher en ce ranc, quelque plus grand' faconde
Le dira. Quant à moy, pour tous je veulx chanter
Les sept costaux Romains, sept miracles du monde.

───────•••───────

Sonnet 2. Du Bellay evokes the wonders of the ancient world: the hanging gardens of Babylon, the temple of Diana at Ephesus, the pyramids, the statue of Zeus at Olympia, the tomb of Mausolus in Caria, the labyrinth of Crete and the colossus of Rhodes. This sonnet illustrates a recurrent feature of his style — use of mutually enriching epithets (here, to suggest pride and grandeur).

Does Babylon here evoke 'the bogey of the feared and hated Roman church', as suggested by Schell in his edition of Spenser's translation? This could hardly have been the intention of Du Bellay: he defends the claims of the Roman Church in the *Antiquitez*, and in the *Songe* he couples allusive criticism of papal corruption with defence of the Roman Church. Even in the *Regrets*, where he attacks the personal lives of popes, he stresses his allegiance to the Catholic faith (in s. 43). He reveals his religious views also in a letter to Jean Du Bellay in defence of the *Regrets* (*Lettres*, in Bellenger, pp. 430–431) and in the *Ample discours au Roy* (in his *Œuvres poétiques*, VI, 189–237). On Du Bellay's religious views, see G. Gadoffre, 'Entre Rome et Genève' (in his *Du Bellay et le sacré*, pp. 183–208), and my *Joachim Du Bellay's veiled victim* (Genève, 1974), pp. 46–57.

~ **2** ~

Great *Babylon* her haughtie walls will praise,
  And sharped steeples high shot up in ayre;
Greece will the olde *Ephesian* buildings blaze,
And *Nylus* nurslings their Pyramides faire;
  The same yet vaunting *Greece* will tell the storie
Of *Joves* great Image in *Olympus* placed;
Mausolus worke will be the *Carians* glorie,
And *Crete* will boast the Labyrinth, now raced;
  The antique *Rhodian* will likewise set forth
The great Colosse, erect to Memorie;
And what els in the world is of like worth,
Some greater learned wit will magnifie.
    But I will sing above all moniments
    Seven *Romane* Hils, the worlds seven wonderments.

The translation. Du Bellay had referred to the hanging gardens of Babylon,
but Spenser alludes to the 'steeples' of Babylon (perhaps in order to hint that
Babylon represents the Church of Rome: we shall see interesting changes,
later, to Du Bellay's endorsements of the Roman Church). Spenser's descrip-
tion of the Cretan labyrinth as 'raced' (razed) has no equivalent in Du Bellay,
and 'above all' (l. 13) mistranslates *pour tous* (= 'instead of all'). Also (for rea-
sons which are uncertain), Du Bellay alternates decasyllabic and alexandrine
lines (until sonnet 31: see my note to the French version of that sonnet), and
Spenser does not convey this distinction.

~ 3 ~

Nouveau venu, qui cherches Rome en Rome
Et rien de Rome en Rome n'apperçois :
Ces vieux palais, ces vieux arcz que tu vois,
Et ces vieux murs, c'est ce que Rome on nomme.
    Voy quel orgueil, quelle ruine :   et comme
Celle qui mist le monde sous ses loix,
Pour donter tout, se donta quelquefois,
Et devint proye au temps, qui tout consomme.
    Rome de Rome est le seul monument,
Et Rome Rome a vaincu seulement.
Le Tybre seul, qui vers la mer s'enfuit,
    Reste de Rome. O mondaine inconstance !
Ce qui est ferme, est par le temps destruit,
Et ce qui fuit, au temps fait resistance.

Sonnet 3. Du Bellay invites the reader to put himself in the position of a perplexed visitor to Rome who cannot find Rome since all is in ruins. Like so many sonnets in the *Antiquitez*, this one justifies the analogy between poetry and painting found in the dedicatory sonnet. Du Bellay's visual material is intended to trigger the reader's imagination and to prompt reflection. Du Bellay also makes demands on the reader's resilience with the paradoxes in lines 1–2, 6–7 and 13–14.
    The sonnet is a translation of an epigram by Janus Vitalis, a Sicilian priest, theologian, poet and courtier of Leo X. Vitalis's poem and Du Bellay's translation of it had a remarkable *fortuna:* I have discovered twenty-eight translations or adaptations of either Vitalis's original or Du Bellay's sonnet in the sixteenth and seventeenth centuries, and many later ones, written in eight languages (see my two articles on Vitalis; see also Tucker, *The poet's Odyssey*, pp. 55–173).

~ 3 ~

Thou stranger, which for *Rome* in *Rome* here seekest,
And nought of *Rome* in *Rome* perceiv'st at all,
These same olde walls, olde arches, which thou seest
Olde Palaces, is that which *Rome* men call.
  Behold what wreake, what ruine, and what wast,
And how that she, which with her mightie powre
Tam'd all the world, hath tam'd herselfe at last,
The pray of time, which all things doth devowre.
  Rome now of *Rome* is th'onely funerall,
And onely *Rome* of *Rome* hath victorie;
Ne ought save *Tyber* hastning to his fall
Remaines of all. 0 worlds inconstancie!
    That which is firme doth flit and fall away,
    And that is flitting, doth abide and stay.

The translation. Spenser loses the antithesis *orgueil/ruine* (l. 5), misses the causal relationship between Rome's destiny and Rome's ruin (ll. 6–7) and omits the references to time (ll. 13–14).

~ **4** ~

Celle qui de son chef les estoilles passoit,
   Et d'un pied sur Thetis, l'autre dessous l'Aurore,
D'une main sur le Scythe, et l'autre sur le More,
De la terre et du ciel la rondeur compassoit,

   Juppiter ayant peur, si plus elle croissoit,
Que l'orgueil des Geans se relevast encore,
L'accabla sous ces monts, ces sept monts qui sont ore
Tumbeaux de la grandeur qui le ciel menassoit.

   Il luy mist sur le chef la croppe Saturnale,
Puis dessus l'estomac assist la Quirinale,
Sur le ventre il planta l'antique Palatin,

   Mist sur la dextre main la hauteur Celienne,
Sur la senestre assist l'eschine Exquilienne,
Viminal sur un pied, sur l'autre l'Aventin.

***

Sonnet 4. Rome bestrode the ancient world, from *Thetis* (a sea-nymph, thus
the Atlantic ocean in the west) to *Aurora* (the goddess of morning, thus the
east), from *Scythia* (the north of Europe) to the land of the *Moors* (Africa
in the south). Du Bellay's subject is thus world dominion — which, in the
dedicatory sonnet, he has presented as the destiny of France. The universal
power of Rome (and, by inference, of France) will be a recurrent theme of the
collection: see s. 6, 8, 16, 22 and 26.

But Rome's aspiration to imperial power, he says, showed hubris. In l. 6,
he evokes the Giants who rebelled against Jupiter and whom Jupiter buried
beneath mountains; Du Bellay cleverly equates these mountains with the
seven hills of Rome. He made the same point in similar terms in the first
of his *Tumuli*, titled *Romæ veteris* (see his *Œuvres poétiques*, VII, pp. 168–169).
On the Giants as a universal symbol of hubris (they recur in this guise in
s. 12), see F. Joukovsky, 'La guerre des dieux et des géants [. . .]', *Bibliothèque
d'Humanisme et Renaissance*, XXIX, 1967, pp. 55–92; on use of the myth by
Du Bellay, see the article by McFarlane, pp. 128–133.

Also in this sonnet, Rome is presented as having a human passion, pride
(l. 6) — and a human body: a head (a *chef*), a foot and a hand. Rome is thus
a macrocosm, and the fate of the city is a warning not just to ambitious states
but also to presumptuous individuals. Repeatedly, Du Bellay will present
Rome in terms applicable to the individual and thus tacitly invite each reader
to engage in self-criticism. There was often a close link in the Renaissance
between poetry and moral philosophy (think of the use Montaigne makes of
poets), and the *Antiquitez* epitomize this link.

~ **4** ~

She, whose high top above the starres did sore,
One foote on *Thetis*, th'other on the Morning,
One hand on *Scythia*, th'other on the *More*,
Both heaven and earth in roundnesse compassing,
    Jove fearing, least if she should greater growe,
The old Giants should once againe uprise,
Her whelm'd with hills, these seven hils, which be nowe
Tombes of her greatnes, which did threate the skies.
    Upon her head he heapt Mount *Saturnal*,
Upon her bellie th'antique *Palatine*,
Upon her stomacke laid Mount *Quirinal*,
On her left hand the noysome *Esquiline*,
    And *Cælian* on the right; but both her feete
    Mount *Viminal* and *Aventine* doo meete.

The translation. Spenser dilutes Du Bellay's plainly deliberate anthropomorphism: he omits any equivalent to the 'head' and the 'pride' of Rome, and translates *eschine Exquilienne* (= 'Esquiline spine': l. 13) by 'noysome Esquiline'. There is no justification in the original for his 'but' in l. 13.

~ **5** ~

Qui voudra voir tout ce qu'ont peu nature,
L'art et le ciel, Rome, te vienne voir,
J'entens s'il peult ta grandeur concevoir
Par ce qui n'est que ta morte peinture.

    Rome n'est plus : et si l'architecture
Quelque umbre encor de Rome fait revoir,
C'est comme un corps par magique sçavoir
Tiré de nuict hors de sa sepulture.

    Le corps de Rome en cendre est devallé,
Et son esprit rejoindre s'est allé
Au grand esprit de ceste masse ronde.

    Mais ses escripts, qui son loz le plus beau
Malgré le temps arrachent du tumbeau,
Font son idole errer parmy le monde.

Sonnet 5. Rome is apparently dead — but it lives on in the writings of the Romans (an echo of s. 1). Here, as in the previous sonnet, Rome is presented anthropomorphically (ll. 9–10): state and individual have a parallel destiny — which includes death. The language of death and burial (*sepulture*, l. 8; *cendre*, l. 9 and *tumbeau*, l. 13) will recur hauntingly in the collection.

    This sonnet begins with an echo of Petrarch's frequently imitated 'Chi vuol veder quantunque può natura' (*Rime*, 248). But unlike other imitators of Petrarch, Du Bellay uses the formula not to extol the beauty of his beloved but to comment on Rome. Before 1558, when Du Bellay published the *Antiquitez* and *Regrets*, the sonnet was associated in France exclusively with love poetry.

~ 5 ~

Who lists to see, what ever nature, arte,
   And heaven could doo, O *Rome*, thee let him see,
In case thy greatnes he can gesse in harte,
By that which but the picture is of thee.
   Rome is no more: but if the shade of *Rome*
May of the bodie yeeld a seeming sight,
It's like a corse drawne forth out of the tombe
By Magicke skill out of eternall night.
   The corpes of *Rome* in ashes is entombed,
And her great spirite rejoyned to the spirite
Of this great masse, is in the same enwombed.
But her brave writings, which her famous merite
   In spight of time, out of the dust doth reare,
   Doo make her Idole through the world appeare.

The translation. Spenser does not translate *morte* (l. 4): this word prepares the quatrain which follows. Spenser's 'if' (l. 5) is concessive, assuming he has understood Du Bellay, whose sense is 'though (=*si*) the city's architecture to this day enables us to glimpse some shadow of Rome, what we see resembles a body drawn at night by magic from its tomb' (ll. 5–8). The remains of the magnificent buildings offer a mere glimmer of the life of a city which is well and truly dead.

~ 6 ~

Telle que dans son char la Berecynthienne
Couronnee de tours, et joyeuse d'avoir
Enfanté tant de Dieux, telle se faisoit voir
En ses jours plus heureux ceste ville ancienne :
    Ceste ville, qui fut plus que la Phrygienne
Foisonnante en enfans, et de qui le pouvoir
Fut le pouvoir du monde, et ne se peult revoir
Pareille à sa grandeur, grandeur sinon la sienne.
    Rome seule pouvoit à Rome ressembler,
Rome seule pouvoit Rome faire trembler :
Aussi n'avoit permis l'ordonnance fatale
    Qu'autre pouvoir humain, tant fust audacieux,
Se vantast d'égaler celle qui fit égale
Sa puissance à la terre et son courage aux cieux.

Sonnet 6. This sonnet echoes the *Aeneid* (VI, 777–787): Romulus rejoiced that his descendants would conquer the world and establish fortified cities, just as Cybele took pride in her numerous divine offspring. Virgil and Du Bellay allude to the fact that Cybele was adored on the Phrygian mountain of Berecyntus and was depicted wearing a crown in the shape of towers (she it was who first taught men to fortify cities). Du Bellay's allusion conjures up the whole scene in the *Aeneid* which describes the imperial destiny of Rome; and the final line of the sonnet echoes, appositely, Virgil's 'Roma / Imperium terris, animos aequabit Olympo'. For Du Bellay's views on imitation of the masterpieces of antiquity, see his *Deffence et illustration de la langue françoyse*, II, iv, v.

~ 6 ~

Such as the *Berecynthian* Goddesse bright
   In her swift charret with high turrets crownde,
Proud that so manie Gods she brought to light —
Such was this Citie in her good daies fownd:
   This Citie, more than that great *Phrygian* mother
Renowm'd for fruite of famous progenie,
Whose greatnes by the greatnes of none other
But by her selfe her equall match could see.
   Rome onely might to *Rome* compared bee,
And onely *Rome* could make great *Rome* to tremble:
So did the Gods by heavenly doome decree,
That other earthlie power should not resemble
      Her that did match the whole earths puissaunce,
      And did her courage to the heavens advaunce.

The translation. Spenser adds material not in Du Bellay: 'Goddesse' (l. 1), 'swift', 'high' (l. 2), 'Renowm'd' (l. 6), 'great' (l. 10). He has no equivalent of *et de qui le pouvoir / Fut le pouvoir du monde* (ll. 6–7) and *tant fust audacieux* (l. 12). 'Proud' (l. 3) is an inexact rendering of *joyeuse;* 'resemble' (l. 12) is only an approximation to *Se vantast d'egaler;* and the concentration of Du Bellay's last line, and its haunting echo of Virgil, is diluted.

~ 7 ~

Sacrez costaux, et vous sainctes ruines,
Qui le seul nom de Rome retenez,
Vieux monuments, qui encor soustenez
L'honneur poudreux de tant d'ames divines,
    Arcz triomphaux, pointes du ciel voisines,
Qui de vous voir le ciel mesme estonnez,
Las, peu à peu cendre vous devenez,
Fable du peuple et publiques rapines!
    Et bien qu'au temps pour un temps facent guerre
Les bastimens, si est-ce que le temps
Œuvres et noms finablement atterre.
    Tristes desirs, vivez donques contents:
Car si le temps finist chose si dure,
Il finira la peine que j'endure.

Sonnet 7. Pagan Rome, even, was sacred — and was guilty of a hubris which
has been punished: the arches and obelisks (l. 5) are rubble and 'spoyle' —
which is now used anew by builders.

Du Bellay's source appears to be the following, by Castiglione:

Superbi colli, e voi, sacre ruine,
Che 'l nome sol di Roma ancor tenete,
Ahi che reliquie miserande avete
Di tant'anime eccelse e pellegrine!
Colossi, archi, teatri, opre divine,
Trionfal pompe gloriose e liete,
In poco cener pur converse siete,
E fatte al vulgo vil favola al fine.
Così se ben un tempo al tempo guerra
Fanno l'opre famose, a passo lento
E l'opre e i nomi il tempo invido atterra.
Vivrò dunque fra' miei martir contento;
Che se il tempo dà fine a ciò ch'è in terra,
Darà forse ancor fine al mio tormento:

On the *fortuna* of Castiglione's sonnet, see J.G. Fucilla, 'Notes sur le sonnet
Superbi colli', *Boletín de la Biblioteca de Menéndez Pelayo*, XXXI, 1955, pp. 51–93.

~ 7 ~

Ye sacred ruines, and ye tragick sights,
  Which onely doo the name of *Rome* retain,
Olde moniments, which of so famous sprights
The honour yet in ashes doo maintaine,
  Triumphant Arcks, spyres neighbours to the skie,
That you to see doth th'heaven it self appall,
Alas, by little ye to nothing flie,
The peoples fable, and the spoyle of all!
  And though your frames do for a time make warre
Gainst time, yet time in time shall ruinate
Your workes and names, and your last reliques marre.
My sad desires, rest therefore moderate:
  For if that time make ende of things so sure,
  It als will end the paine, which I endure.

The translation. In the first quatrain, Du Bellay uses three religious epithets to describe Rome (*Sacrez costaux* [...] *sainctes ruines* [...] *ames divines*): he seems to be preparing the point, hinted at in the next sonnet, and explicit in s. 18, that Rome acquired a religious authority which replaced its political power. Spenser renders only one of these three epithets by a term suggesting the sacred. His statement that time will 'your last reliques marre' (l. 11) has no equivalent in the original.

~ 8 ~

Par armes et vaisseaux Rome donta le monde,
Et pouvoit on juger qu'une seule cité
Avoit de sa grandeur le terme limité
Par la mesme rondeur de la terre et de l'onde.

Et tant fut la vertu de ce peuple feconde
En vertueux nepveux, que sa posterité
Surmontant ses ayeux en brave auctorité,
Mesura le hault ciel à la terre profonde :

Afin qu'ayant rangé tout pouvoir sous sa main,
Rien ne peust estre borne à l'empire Romain,
Et que, si bien le temps destruit les Republiques,

Le temps ne mist si bas la Romaine hauteur,
Que le chef deterré aux fondemens antiques,
Qui prindrent nom de luy, fust découvert menteur.

Sonnet 8. The political power of the ancient Romans covered the earth (ll. 1–4)
— and their descendants (*nepveux*, l. 6) claim a heavenly power equal to the
earthly power of the ancient Romans (ll. 7–8) — an allusion to the universal
jurisdiction of the Roman Church. That this is Du Bellay's point is confirmed
by lines 9 and 10 (Rome has enjoyed all power that there is, and there are
no limits to the sway of Rome) and by the conclusion: time destroys political
communities, but Rome remains the 'head' of humanity. The idea that Roman
authority persists but now resides in the Church is found again in s. 17 and
18. It is ancient: *si non manet civitas quæ nos carnaliter genuit, manet quæ nos
spiritualiter genuit* ('the city which gave us birth according to the flesh no
longer remains, but there remains the city which gave us birth according to
the spirit' — St. Augustine: see Garaud, p. 154; see also a note to s. 18 below).

Du Bellay's conclusion alludes to the story (recorded by Plutarch in *Camil-
lus*, XXXI) that a newly-severed head was discovered when foundations were
being dug for the Capitol, and that this was interpreted as an augury that the
place was to become the head of Italy. Du Bellay suggests that this head (*ca-
put*) gave the Capitol its name. His source may be J.B. Marliani's *Topographiæ
veteris Romæ Epitome* (see Saulnier, pp. 115–118).

~ 8 ~

Through armes and vassals *Rome* the world subdu'd,
   That one would weene, that one sole Cities strength
Both land and sea in roundes had survew'd,
To be the measure of her bredth and length.
   This peoples vertue yet so fruitfull was
Of vertuous nephewes, that posteritie
Striving in power their grandfathers to passe,
The lowest earth, join'd to the heaven hie:
   To th'end that having all parts in their power,
Nought from the Romane Empire might be quight,
And that though time doth Commonwealths devowre,
Yet no time should so low embase their hight,
   That her head earth'd in her foundations deep,
   Should not her name and endles honour keep.

The translation. Du Bellay states (paraphrasing him, to make l. 8 intelligible) that the descendants of the ancient Romans, 'surpassing their forbears in lofty authority, made their celestial power as extensive as the earth itself'. The ancient Romans, in other words, enjoyed political sway and their posterity added religious authority. Spenser blurs this point — perhaps through lack of sympathy with it. See the note to s. 17.

~ 9 ~

Astres cruelz, et vous Dieux inhumains,
Ciel envieux, et marastre Nature,
Soit que par ordre ou soit qu'à l'aventure
Voyse le cours des affaires humains,
 Pourquoy jadis ont travaillé voz mains
A façonner ce monde qui tant dure?
Ou que ne fut de matiere aussi dure
Le brave front de ces palais Romains?
 Je ne dy plus la sentence commune,
Que toute chose au dessous de la Lune
Est corrompable et sugette à mourir:
 Mais bien je dy (et n'en veuille desplaire
A qui s'efforce enseigner le contraire)
Que ce grand Tout doit quelquefois perir.

Sonnet 9. 'Why', Du Bellay plaintively asks the stars, the gods, heaven and nature, 'did you make a world which outlived Rome? Or (to put the question another way) why did you not make Rome as durable as the world?' The conclusion, in the tercets, is that the world itself is mortal. This was a common reflection (*in una urbe totus orbis interiit:* 'as one city was ruined, so too was the whole world' — St. Jerome: see Garaud, p. 154; on the destruction of Rome and the end of the world, see also below, s. 20 and 22). In concluding that the world is mortal, Du Bellay is refuting contemporary Italian followers of Averroes: see G. Gadoffre, *Du Bellay et le sacré*, Paris, 1978, pp. 141–144.

~ 9 ~

Ye cruell starres, and eke ye Gods unkinde,
 Heaven envious, and bitter stepdame Nature,
Be it by fortune, or by course of kinde
That ye doo weld th'affaires of earthlie creature,
    Why have your hands long sithence traveiled
To frame this world, that doth endure so long?
Or why were not these Romane palaces
Made of some matter no lesse firme and strong?
    I say not, as the common voyce doth say,
That all things which beneath the Moone have being
Are temporall, and subject to decay:
But I say rather, though not all agreeing
    With some, that weene the contrarie in thought,
    That all this whole shall one day come to nought.

The translation. Spenser's 'by course of kind' (l. 3) (glossed by Schell as 'in the normal course of nature') must correspond to Du Bellay's *par ordre*. Spenser has not quite rendered the parenthetical remark in lines 12–13: 'I would not wish to antagonize anyone who seeks to teach the contrary'.

~ **10** ~

Plus qu'aux bords Aëteans le brave filz d'Aeson
Qui par enchantement conquist la riche laine,
Des dents d'un vieil serpent ensemençant la plaine
N'engendra de soldatz au champ de la toison,
      Ceste ville, qui fut en sa jeune saison
Un Hydre de guerriers, se vid bravement pleine
De braves nourrissons, dont la gloire hautaine
A remply du Soleil l'une et l'autre maison :
      Mais qui finablement, ne se trouvant au monde
Hercule qui dontast semence tant feconde,
D'une horrible fureur l'un contre l'autre armez,
      Se moissonnarent tous par un soudain orage,
Renouvelant entre eulx la fraternelle rage
Qui aveugla jadis les fiers soldats semez.

Sonnet 10. Jason slew a dragon and scattered its teeth — whereupon armed warriors sprang up from the ground and slew each other. Du Bellay presents the fable (recounted by Ovid in *Metamorphoses*, VII, 121–131) as a warning of civil war. The analogous myth of Cadmus, who also sowed a dragon's teeth and, when armed warriors sprang up, had them fight each other (Ovid, *Metamorphoses*, III, 101–126) has long been seen as a symbol of civil war: see Lucan, *Pharsalia*, IV, 549–556.

In the dedicatory sonnet, Du Bellay presented his work as a prefiguration of French universal power. But by the time the *Antiquitez* appeared in 1558 there was a clear possibility that religious dissidence would lead to civil strife in France. Du Bellay seems to be implicitly inviting the nation to choose between world dominion, as enjoyed by Rome, and annihilation through civil war — which had also been the fate of Rome. After the death of Du Bellay (in 1560), civil war broke out in France — and Ronsard then echoed much of Du Bellay's material on Rome in deploring the war (he twice used the myths of earth-born warriors: see my edition of his *Discours des miseres*, Genève, 1979, p. 83, 246–247).

In line 8, *Du Soleil l'une et l'autre maison* echoes Ovid's 'Solis utramque domum' (*Heroïdes*, IX, 16) and means 'east and west': the exploits of the Romans enjoy worldwide fame.

~ 10 ~

A s that brave sonne of *Aeson*, which by charmes
Atcheiv'd the golden Fleece in *Colchid* land,
Out of the earth engendred men of armes
Of Dragons teeth, sowne in the sacred sand,
　So this brave Towne, that in her youthlie daies
An *Hydra* was of warriours glorious,
Did fill with her renowmed nourslings praise
The firie sunnes both one and other hous:
　But they at last, there being then not living
An *Hercules*, so ranke seed to represse,
Emongst themselves with cruell furie striving,
Mow'd downe themselves with slaughter mercilesse,
　　Renewing in themselves that rage unkinde,
　　Which whilom did those earthborn brethren blinde.

The translation. Spenser's 'sacred' (l. 4) is an embellishment, and 'cruell furie' (l. 11) is only approximate to *soudain orage*. In the conclusion, there is no equivalent in Spenser for *fiers soldatz* (or in Du Bellay for 'unkinde').

~ 11 ~

Mars vergongneux d'avoir donné tant d'heur
A ses nepveux, que l'impuissance humaine
Enorgueillie en l'audace Romaine
Sembloit fouler la celeste grandeur,
  Refroidissant ceste premiere ardeur,
Dont le Romain avoit l'ame si pleine,
Souffla son feu, et d'une ardente haleine
Vint eschauffer la Gottique froideur.
  Ce peuple adonc, nouveau fils de la Terre,
Dardant par tout les fouldres de la guerre,
Ces braves murs accabla sous sa main,
  Puis se perdit dans le sein de sa mere,
Affin que nul, fust-ce des Dieux le pere,
Se peust vanter de l'empire Romain.

Sonnet 11. A sequel to the previous sonnet and (like many of the sonnets in the *Antiquitez*) a miniature narrative poem. Mars saw that Rome was becoming presumptuous, and conjured up a new race of earth-born warriors, the Goths, to destroy Rome; and the victors then vanished without trace back into the bosom of the earth, lest anyone survive who could lay claim to the dominion (*empire*, l. 14) enjoyed by Rome. Another sonnet showing the fate of hubris.

Du Bellay's term *fils de la Terre* (l. 9) echoes a classical commonplace: the term *Terræ filius* designated a man of humble and obscure origin (since, as Erasmus explained in his *Adagia*, I, viii, 86, the Earth is the common parent of us all). In the present context, therefore, *Fils de la terre* suggests presumption (see the note by Michael Heath).

~ 11 ~

M^{*ars*} shaming to have given so great head
To his off-spring, that mortall puissaunce
Puft up with pride of Romane hardiehead,
Seem'd above heavens powre it selfe to advance,
  Cooling againe his former kindled heate,
With which he had those Romane spirits fild,
Did blowe new fire, and with enflamed breath,
Into the Gothicke colde hot rage instil'd.
  Then gan that Nation, th'earths new Giant brood,
To dart abroad the thunder bolts of warre,
And beating downe these walls with furious mood
Into her mothers bosome, all did marre,
  To th'end that none, all were it *Jove* his sire
  Should boast himselfe of the Romane Empire.

───────◆●◆───────

The translation. 'Mortall puissance' (l. 2) is only an approximate rendering (if that) of *impuissance humaine*. 'Abroad' (which meant 'widely'; l. 10) is a weak rendering of *par tout* ('everywhere'). In l. 11, Spenser has transferred the epithet *braves* ('haughty', 'arrogant') from the walls of Rome to the Goths and rendered it loosely as 'with furious mood'. *Puis se perdit* (l. 12: 'then disappeared'): Du Bellay has the Goths vanish back into the earth, Spenser has them destroy the city of Rome and bury it. 'Jove his sire' (l. 13): i.e. the father of Jove, Saturn (Du Bellay had referred, less specifically, to 'the father of the gods'). The last two lines of Du Bellay must mean 'lest there should be anyone able to boast that he enjoyed the universal power Rome once had'.

~ **12** ~

Telz que lon vid jadis les enfans de la Terre
Plantez dessus les monts pour escheller les cieux,
Combattre main à main la puissance des Dieux,
Et Juppiter contre eux, qui ses fouldres desserre,
    Puis tout soudainement renversez du tonnerre
Tumber deça dela ces squadrons furieux,
La Terre gemissante, et le Ciel glorieux
D'avoir à son honneur achevé ceste guerre :
    Tel encor' on a veu par dessus les humains
Le front audacieux des sept costaux Romains
Lever contre le ciel son orgueilleuse face.
    Et telz ores on void ces champs deshonnorez
Regretter leur ruine, et les Dieux asseurez
Ne craindre plus là hault si effroyable audace.

Sonnet 12. The 'children of the earth' this time are the Giants, who sprang
from the blood of Uranus when it fell upon the earth (so that Gaea, the earth,
is their mother); the Giants, as Du Bellay recalls here, piled mountains on
each other in an attempt to scale heaven. This time, it is the Romans who are
compared to an earth-born race: for, stationed on the seven hills, they proudly
challenged heaven — and, like the Giants, they have been punished for pride.
Du Bellay applied this myth to Rome in s. 4; see also s. 17 and *Songe*, s. 15.

As often, Du Bellay uses the 'architecture' of the sonnet to project his point:
here, each quatrain and tercet corresponds to a stage in the story, and the
structure is underlined by repetition of *tel*. Du Bellay compared poetry to
architecture in s. 25, below (see the note to that sonnet).

Also typically, the language carries a strong moral resonance, and an inti-
mation that what applies to the state can apply to the individual — for, as
well as moral attributes, the city has a *front audacieux*, an arrogant brow. We
have seen parallels between the fate of Rome and the fate of the individual
in s. 4 and 5.

~ **12** ~

Like as whilome the children of the earth
Heapt hils on hils, to scale the starrie skie,
And fight against the Gods of heavenly berth,
Whiles *Jove* at them his thunderbolts let flie,
   All suddenly with lightning overthrowne,
The furious squadrons downe to ground did fall,
That th'earth under her childrens weight did grone,
And th'heavens in glorie triumpht over all:
   So did that haughtie front which heaped was
On these seven Romane hils, it selfe upreare
Over the world, and lift her loftie face
Against the heaven, that gan her force to feare.
   But now these scorned fields bemone her fall,
   And Gods secure feare not her force at all.

The translation. Spenser's 'of heavenly berth' (l. 3) is otiose as an epithet for gods, and does not render *la puissance des Dieux*. Du Bellay's *La Terre gemissante* (l. 7) suggests to me that the Earth was mourning the defeat of her offspring rather than (as Spenser has it) groaning under their weight. Spenser does not convey the tight structure of the poem, nor the impact which Du Bellay achieves with his two last words.

~ **13** ~

Ny la fureur de la flamme enragee,
Ny le trenchant du fer victorieux,
Ny le degast du soldat furieux,
Qui tant de fois, Rome, t'a saccagee,
   Ny coup sur coup ta fortune changee,
Ny le ronger des siecles envieux,
Ny le despit des hommes et des Dieux,
Ny contre toy ta puissance rangee,
   Ny l'esbranler des vents impetueux,
Ny le débord de ce Dieu tortueux,
Qui tant de fois t'a couvert de son onde,
   Ont tellement ton orgueil abbaissé,
Que la grandeur du rien qu'ilz t'ont laissé
Ne face encor' emerveiller le monde.

Sonnet 13. The anaphora focuses attention on the last lines — and clever lines: Rome's pride has been humbled, but to this day the grandeur of the nothing that is Rome amazes the world.

~ 13 ~

Nor the swift furie of the flames aspiring,
  Nor the deep wounds of victours raging blade,
Nor ruthlesse spoyle of souldiers blood-desiring,
The which so oft thee (*Rome*) their conquest made,
    Ne stroke on stroke of fortune variable,
Ne rust of age hating continuance,
Nor wrath of Gods, nor spight of men unstable,
Nor thou opposd' against thine owne puissance,
    Nor th'horrible uprore of windes high blowing,
Nor swelling streames of that God snakie-paced,
Which hath so often with his overflowing
Thee drenched, have thy pride so much abaced,
    But that this nothing, which they have thee left,
    Makes the world wonder, what they from thee reft.

The translation. In l. 6, 'rust' is an imaginative rendering of *le ronger* ('gnaw-ing'); so too is 'snakie-paced' (l. 10) for Du Bellay's *tortueux* ('meandering'; referring to the Tiber). Du Bellay's l. 7 means 'Nor the spite of men and gods'. In the conclusion to the sonnet, Du Bellay stands in awe even at the nothingness to which Rome is now reduced; Spenser wonders at what Rome must once have been.

~ 14 ~

Comme on passe en aesté le torrent sans danger,
Qui souloit en hyver estre roy de la plaine,
Et ravir par les champs d'une fuite hautaine
L'espoir du laboureur et l'espoir du berger;

Comme on void les coüards animaux oultrager
Le courageux lion gisant dessus l'arene,
Ensanglanter leurs dents, et d'une audace vaine
Provoquer l'ennemy qui ne se peult venger;

Et comme devant Troye on vid des Grecz encor
Braver les moins vaillans autour du corps d'Hector:
Ainsi ceulx qui jadis souloient, à teste basse,

Du triomphe Romain la gloire accompagner,
Sur ces poudreux tumbeaux exercent leur audace,
Et osent les vaincuz les vainqueurs desdaigner.

Sonnet 14. Du Bellay's point is that we should not speak ill of ancient Rome. His source may be an emblem by Andrea Alciati. Each of Alciati's emblems consists in a title (which is often a proverb), a picture and an epigram; these three elements are mutually illuminating and point to a moral truth (Du Bellay's *Antiquitez*, with their use of proverbs, their visual content and their frequently epigrammatic nature, are strikingly reminiscent of the emblem). In emblem 153, Alciati's proverb is *Cum larvis non luctandum*, 'We ought not to attack the dead'; his picture is of hares pulling at the beard of a dead lion (an allusion to the proverb 'Mortuo leoni et lepures insultant', recorded by Erasmus in *Adagia*, IV, vii, 82); and his epigram, echoing the *Iliad* (XXII, 369–375), shows the wounded Hector reproaching lesser warriors who insult him:

Aeacidae moriens percussu cuspidis Hector
Qui toties hosteis vicerat ante suos
Comprimere haud potuit vocem insultantibus illis,
Dum curru et pedibus nectere vincla parant:
'Distrahite ut libitum est: sic cassi leonis
Convellunt barbam vel timidi lepores'.

To this material, Du Bellay has added the image of the stream, which appears to be derived from Ariosto's *Orlando furioso* (XXXVIII, 110).

The conclusion may hint at the sack of Rome by the imperial troops in 1527.

~ 14 ~

As men in Summer fearles passe the foord,
Which is in Winter lord of all the plaine,
And with his tumbling streames doth beare aboord
The ploughmans hope, and shepheards labour vaine;
    And as the coward beasts use to despise
The noble Lion after his lives end,
Whetting their teeth, and with vaine foolhardise
Daring the foe, that cannot him defend;
    And as at *Troy* most dastards of the Greekes
Did brave about the corpes of *Hector* colde;
So those which whilome wont with pallid cheekes
The Romane triumphs glorie to behold,
        Now on these ashie tombes shew boldnesse vaine,
        And conquer'd dare the Conquerour disdaine.

***

The translation. Spenser has not conveyed the *hautaine* (= 'arrogant', 'aloof') of line 3; *gisant dessus l'arene* (l. 6) means 'lying in the sand'; in ll. 9–10, Du Bellay says 'And, again, as we saw Greeks before Troy defying less valiant warriors, as Hector lay dead'; lines 11–12 of Du Bellay refer to those defeated foes of Rome who were made to march under the yoke in acknowledgement of their defeat.

~ 15 ~

Palles Esprits, et vous Umbres poudreuses,
    Qui jouissant de la clarté du jour
Fistes sortir cest orgueilleux sejour,
Dont nous voyons les reliques cendreuses:
    Dictes, Esprits (ainsi les tenebreuses
Rives de Styx non passable au retour,
Vous enlaçant d'un trois fois triple tour,
N'enferment point voz images umbreuses),
    Dictes moy donc (car quelqu'une de vous
Possible encore se cache icy dessous)
Ne sentez vous augmenter vostre peine,
    Quand quelquefois de ces costaux Romains
Vous contemplez l'ouvrage de voz mains
N'estre plus rien qu'une poudreuse plaine?

———●◆●———

Sonnet 15. Du Bellay asks the spirits of the builders of ancient Rome (who are now trapped on the banks of the river Styx: an echo of Virgil's *Aeneid*, VI, 425, 'ripam irremeabilis undæ' and 439, 'novies Styx interfusa coercet') what they feel when they see their lofty buildings reduced to dust. It is only at the end of the sonnet that he gets round to putting this question, for he knows it will cause anguish to the spirits to whom it is addressed. For a discussion of analogous texts, see Tucker, *The poet's Odyssey*, pp. 214–224.

~ 15 ~

Ye pallid spirits, and ye ashie ghoasts,
 Which joying in the brightnes of your day,
Brought foorth those signes of your presumptuous boasts
Which now their dusty reliques do bewray:
    Tell me ye spirits (sith the darksome river
Of Styx, not passable to soules returning,
Enclosing you in thrice three wards for ever,
Doo not restraine your images still mourning),
    Tell me then (for perhaps some one of you
Yet here above him secretly doth hide)
Doo ye not feele your torments to accrewe,
When ye sometimes behold the ruin'd pride
        Of these old *Romane* works built with your hands,
        Now to become nought els, but heaped sands?

The translation. Du Bellay's first quatrain, literally translated, runs: 'Pale spirits and ashen shades who, whilst you enjoyed the light of day, constructed this proud abode of which we see the dusty relics'. Spenser's 'bewray' (l. 4) means to expose or reveal, often with the suggestion that what is exposed is discreditable; this latter nuance is not present in Du Bellay. The sense of Du Bellay's second quatrain is that while the spirits of the ancient Romans are trapped in the underworld, their *images umbreuses* ('shadowy images'; rendered by Spenser as 'images still mourning') can escape and appear to the poet. In l. 10, Du Bellay evokes the possibility that one of the Roman builders lies *icy dessous*, beneath his very feet: Spenser has read *dessus* for *dessous!* Du Bellay's *de ces costaux Romains* (l. 12: 'from these Roman hillsides') is not conveyed; Spenser's 'the ruin'd pride' (l. 12) is an elaboration, as is 'heaped sands' (l. 14). The point of Du Bellay's *poudreuse plaine* (l. 14 — an eloquent conclusion to the sonnet) is that the buildings which once soared aloft have been flattened.

~ **16** ~

Comme l'on void de loing sur la mer courroucee
Une montaigne d'eau d'un grand branle ondoyant,
Puis trainant mille flotz, d'un gros choc abboyant
Se crever contre un roc, où le vent l'a poussee;
    Comme on void la fureur par l'Aquilon chassee
D'un sifflement aigu l'orage tournoyant,
Puis d'une aile plus large en l'air s'esbanoyant
Arrester tout à coup sa carriere lassee;
    Et comme on void la flamme ondoyant en cent lieux
Se rassemblant en un, s'aguiser vers les cieux,
Puis tumber languissante: ainsi parmy le monde
    Erra la Monarchie, et croissant tout ainsi
Qu'un flot, qu'un vent, qu'un feu, sa course vagabonde
Par un arrest fatal s'est venuë perdre icy.

Sonnet 16. This sonnet, like many others (see the note to s. 12), is remarkable for its structure. Du Bellay's similes articulate the point that universal dominion came inevitably to Rome — and inevitably ended there. Each simile describes a phenomenon which dominates one of the elements (water, air and fire) — and the phenomenon which dominates the fourth element, the earth, is Rome's *monarchie* (universal power). Each simile is contained within one of the divisions of the sonnet, and each is introduced by the same clause; and the structure is tightened by recall of the three similes in l. 13. Du Bellay's first simile, of the wave gathering momentum, possibly echoes Virgil (*Aeneid*, VII, 528–530 or *Georgics*, III, 237–240) — who was himself echoing Homer (*Iliad*, IV, 422–425).

~ 16 ~

Like as ye see the wrathfull Sea from farre,
    In a great mountaine heap't with hideous noyse,
Eftsoones of thousand billowes shouldred narre,
Against a Rocke to breake with dreadfull poyse;
    Like as ye see fell *Boreas* with sharpe blast,
Tossing huge tempests through the troubled skie,
Eftsoones having his wide wings spent in wast,
To stop his wearie cariere suddenly;
    And as ye see huge flames spred diverslie,
Gathered in one up to the heavens to spyre,
Eftsoones consum'd to fall downe feebily:
So whilom did this Monarchie aspyre
      As waves, as winde, as fire spred over all,
      Till it by fatall doome adowne did fall.

The translation. Du Bellay's *branle* (l. 2) suggests 'stirring' (not 'noise'); Spenser's 'shouldred narre' (l. 3) means 'pushed near'. *Où le vent l'a poussée* (l. 4) means 'where the wind has driven it'. Du Bellay's lines 5–8 mean 'As you see Boreas driving the frenzied elements and whipping the storm into a whirlwind with a sharp whine, then with a broader wing playfully disporting himself in the air and suddenly bringing his weary career to a halt'. Spenser loses much of the impact of the original: Du Bellay is saying that just as a tidal wave, a storm and a conflagration all reach a culminating point, so too does supreme power, which reached its culmination in Rome — and there collapsed abruptly. This sonnet prepares the next two, where Du Bellay shows what has become of Rome's power.

~ **17** ~

Tant que l'oyseau de Juppiter vola,
  Portant le feu dont le ciel nous menace,
Le ciel n'eut peur de l'effroyable audace
Qui des Geans le courage affolla.

  Mais aussi tost que le Soleil brusla
L'aile qui trop se feit la terre basse,
La terre mist hors de sa lourde masse
L'antique horreur qui le droit viola.

  Alors on vid la corneille Germaine
Se deguisant feindre l'aigle Romaine,
Et vers le ciel s'eslever de rechef

  Ces braves monts autrefois mis en poudre,
Ne voyant plus voler dessus leur chef
Ce grand oyseau ministre de la foudre.

Sonnet 17. The Roman eagle, symbol of divine authority, flew too high and
was burned by the sun; and the authority of the Roman eagle is now mimicked
by the German rook. The sense may be that the authority of the Holy Roman
Empire, that is of Germany, a great rival of France, is a pale reflection of
ancient Rome; the dedicatory sonnet to Henry II, which evokes the French
monarch's aspiration to universal power, would support this interpretation.

But a better explanation is that Du Bellay is referring to the Church of
Rome. The authority in question here comes from heaven, and it held the
Giants in check (the Giants were often used as symbols of heretics: see the
article by Joukovsky referred to in the note to s. 4). But now the presumption
and hubris of the popes has lost them their credibility, and their power has
been mimicked by Luther, the 'German rook' of l. 9. This explanation fits the
content and the context (for it follows logically from s. 16 and prepares s. 18)
— and it fits Du Bellay's religious opinions, for he deplored papal corruption
yet regarded the Reformers as heretical.

~ 17 ~

So long as *Joves* great Bird did make his flight,
Bearing the fire with which heaven doth us fray,
Heaven had not feare of that presumptuous might,
With which the Giaunts did the Gods assay.
    But all so soone, as scortching Sunne had brent
His wings, which wont the earth to overspredd,
The earth out of her massie wombe forth sent
That antique horror, which made heaven adredd.
    Then was the Germane Raven in disguise
That Romane Eagle seene to cleave asunder,
And towards heaven freshly to arise
Out of these mountaines, now consum'd to pouder,
    In which the foule that serves to beare the lightning,
    Is now no more seen flying, nor alighting.

The translation. There are minor alterations in the quatrains but, much more importantly, Spenser has completely altered the tercets, which in the original read: 'Then was seen the German rook disguising itself and mimicking the Roman eagle, and these lofty mountains, once reduced to rubble, rise again towards heaven, since they no longer saw this great bird, the minister of [Jupiter's] lightning, flying above their head'. Thus, the Germans offer a derisory parody of the authority of Rome and, like the Giants of old who piled mountains on each other to scale heaven, they are rebelling against divine authority. In Spenser, the German destroys the power of Rome rather than mimicking it (Spenser may have confused *feindre* with *fendre*), and then soars aloft above the ashes of Rome towards heaven. It seems likely that the reason Spenser altered the poem is that he saw Du Bellay was attacking the Lutherans (or that at any rate the poem lends itself to that interpretation). Spenser frequently blurs or removes material sympathetic to the Church of Rome or hostile to the Reformation: see s. 2, 7, 8, 26, 28 and *L'envoy*; also *Songe*, s. 12 and 13, and my notes to these poems. The translation of the next sonnet, however, is an exception to this phenomenon. His alterations to Du Bellay's theology are much more numerous than has been noticed (though see the note to s. 28).

~ 18 ~

Ces grands monceaux pierreux, ces vieux murs que tu vois,
 Furent premierement le cloz d'un lieu champestre,
Et ces braves palais, dont le temps s'est fait maistre,
Cassines de pasteurs ont esté quelquefois.

Lors prindrent les bergers les ornemens des Roys,
Et le dur laboureur de fer arma sa dextre ;
Puis l'annuel pouvoir le plus grand se vid estre,
Et fut encor plus grand le pouvoir de six mois,

 Qui, fait perpetuel, creut en telle puissance,
Que l'aigle Imperial de luy print sa naissance.
Mais le Ciel s'opposant à tel accroissement,

 Mist ce pouvoir es mains du successeur de Pierre,
Qui sous nom de pasteur, fatal à ceste terre,
Monstre que tout retourne à son commencement.

Sonnet 18. Another miniature narrative poem (the temporal adverbs underline the historical development): the site of Rome was originally the fields of pastors, who were succeeded by kings, consuls (l. 7), dictators (l. 8) and emperors, until heaven placed the power of Rome in the hands of the bishop of Rome — a pastor once again. As in s. 8 and, probably, s. 17, Roman political authority has been superseded by religious jurisdiction. Lines 11–14 of Du Bellay's sonnet were cited by Florimond de Raemond, the historian, religious controversialist and friend of Montaigne, in a collection of tributes to the Roman Catholic Church (see his *L'Anti-Christ*, 1597, B.L. 3902 bbb 24).

The notion that Roman religious jurisdiction has replaced Roman political power is in St. Augustine (see note to s. 8). It is found in others who reflected on the ruins of Rome: Dante (*Letters*, ed. P. Toynbee, nos. 5, 6, 7 and *Inferno*, II, 19–24); Jean Dorat (see Geneviève Demerson, *Dorat en son temps*, Clermont-Ferrand, 1983, p. 142); Jean-Antoine de Baïf (see Roubichou-Stretz, *Vision de l'histoire*, p. 34); Quevedo (see R.J. Cuervo, 'Dos poesías de Quevedo a Roma', *Revue hispanique*, XVIII, 1908, pp. 432–438). A variant on this 'Catholic' vision of Rome's destiny is the view of George Buchanan, echoed by Jacques Grévin and Innocent Gentillet: that the ancient Romans conquered the earth, the first bishops of Rome won heaven — and that the realm of the present day popes is hell. See L. Sozzi, 'La polémique anti-italienne en France au XVIe siècle', *Atti della Accademia delle Scienze di Torino*, II, Classe di Scienze morali, storiche e filologiche, CVI, 1971–72 (pp. 99–190), pp. 172–175.

~ **18** ~

These heapes of stones, these old wals which ye see,
 Were first enclosures but of salvage soyle,
And these brave Pallaces which maystred bee
Of time, were shepheards cottages somewhile.
 Then tooke the shepheards Kingly ornaments
And the stout hynde arm'd his right hand with steele;
Eftsoones their rule of yearely Presidents
Grew great, and six months greater a great deele,
 Which made perpetuall, rose to so great might,
That thence th'Imperiall Eagle rooting tooke —
Till th'heaven it selfe opposing gainst her might,
Her power to *Peters* successor betooke,
 Who shepheardlike (as fates the same foreseeing)
 Doth shew, that all things turne to their first being.

The translation. Interestingly, this unequivocally 'Catholic' sonnet of Du Bellay's is one of those most faithfully translated by Spenser. At first sight, this is curious in view of his systematic suppression elsewhere of Du Bellay's endorsements of papal authority (see the note to the previous sonnet). However, Spenser doubtless saw that the notion of the popes as shepherds was the very basis of the sonnet and could not be omitted.

~ **19** ~

Tout le parfait dont le ciel nous honnore,
Tout l'imparfait qui naist dessous les cieux,
Tout ce qui paist noz esprits et noz yeux,
Et tout cela qui noz plaisirs devore,
    Tout le malheur qui nostre aage dedore,
Tout le bon heur des siecles les plus vieux,
Rome du temps de ses premiers ayeux
Le tenoit clos, ainsi qu'une Pandore.
    Mais le Destin debrouillant ce Chaos,
Où tout le bien et le mal fut enclos,
A fait depuis que les vertus divines
    Volant au ciel ont laissé les pechez,
Qui jusqu'icy se sont tenus cachez
Sous les monceaux de ces vieilles ruines.

Sonnet 19. A sonnet which (very unusually for the *Antiquitez*) borders on the satirical (the content is not dissimilar to that of *Regrets*, s. 78). Ancient Rome contained all that is good and evil: but the virtues have returned to heaven while the vices, hitherto contained beneath the ruins, are now manifest.

Pandora (l. 8), the first woman, was sent by Zeus to afflict mankind after Prometheus stole Zeus's fire from heaven. She brought from heaven a box containing every human ill; when the box was opened, they spread over the earth; only hope remained (see Plutarch's quotation from Hesiod in *A letter to Apollonius*, 105). In a later version of the story, the box contains all blessings; when Pandora opened the box, they all flew away. According to Gadoffre (*Du Bellay et le sacré*, pp. 132–135), Du Bellay's Pandora represents Eve; the suggestion is plausible, for the poet hints elsewhere at the Judæo-Christian counterparts of classical myth (in s. 4 the story of the Giants recalls that of Babel, and in s. 24 the *vieil peché* of Romulus possibly suggests original sin).

~ 19 ~

All that is perfect, which th'heaven beautefies;
All that's imperfect, borne belowe the Moone;
All that doth feede our spirits and our eies,
And all that doth consume our pleasures soone,
    All the mishap, the which our daies outweares,
All the good hap of th'oldest times afore,
Rome in the time of her great ancesters,
Like a *Pandora*, locked long in store.
    But destinie this huge *Chaos* turmoyling,
In which all good and evill was enclosed,
Their heavenly vertues from these woes assoyling,
Caried to heaven, from sinfall bondage losed:
        But their great sinnes, the causers of their paine,
        Under these antique ruines yet remaine.

The translation. Spenser does not render Du Bellay's *dedorer* (l. 5), 'to take the gilt off' (an allusion to the Golden Age, the primeval state of innocence described by ancient poets). Du Bellay's *debrouillant* (l. 9) indicates that Destiny disentangled the confused mixture of virtues and vices (Spenser's 'turmoyling', meaning 'agitating', 'disturbing', 'troubling', is not an accurate rendering). Spenser's 'assoyling' (l. 11) means 'setting free'. The insinuation in Du Bellay's *jusqu'icy se sont tenus cachez* (l. 13) is that vice in Rome has in recent times become shamelessly overt — a nuance not conveyed by Spenser.

~ **20** ~

Non autrement qu'on void la pluvieuse nüe
Des vapeurs de la terre en l'air se soulever,
Puis se courbant en arc, à fin de s'abrever,
Se plonger dans le sein de Thetis la chenue,
 Et montant de rechef d'où elle estoit venue,
Sous un grand ventre obscur tout le monde couver,
Tant que finablement on la void se crever,
Or' en pluie, or' en neige, or' en gresle menue :
 Ceste ville qui fut l'ouvrage d'un pasteur,
S'elevant peu à peu, creut en telle hauteur,
Que royne elle se vid de la terre et de l'onde,
 Tant que ne pouvant plus si grand faix soustenir,
Son pouvoir dissipé s'écarta par le monde,
Monstrant que tout en rien doit un jour devenir.

Sonnet 20. As a cloud gathers, then plunges to the sea (Thetis was a deity of the sea) and broods over the whole earth, and then disperses, Rome gathered strength and then dissipated that strength — showing that all things will come to an end. Line 6 offers a simile within the simile, and a graphic one. The view that the fall of Rome portends the end of the world is seen also in s. 9 and 22.

~ 20 ~

No otherwise than raynie cloud, first fed
With earthly vapours gathered in the ayre,
Eftsoones in compas arch't, to steepe his hed,
Doth plonge himselle in *Tethys* bosome faire,
    And mounting up againe, from whence he came,
With his great bellie spreds the dimmed world,
Till at the last dissolving his moist frame,
In raine, or snowe, or haile he forth is horld:
    This Citie, which was first but shepheards shade,
Uprising by degrees, grewe to such height
That Queene of land and sea her selfe she made.
At last not able to beare so great weight,
    Her power disperst, through all the world did vade,
    To shew that all in th'end to nought shall fade.

The translation. The contrast between the rise and the fall of the cloud (ll. 1–4) is less clear in Spenser. Spenser also confuses Du Bellay's Thetis, wife of Peleus and mother of Achilles, with another sea deity, Tethys, wife of Oceanus (as others did at the time). The point of l. 6 is that the 'belly' of the cloud covers the whole earth — an allusion to universal power which is none too clear in Spenser. Spenser's 'vade' (l. 13) means 'pass away', 'perish'.

~ **21** ~

Celle que Pyrrhe et le Mars de Libye
N'ont sceu donter, celle brave cité
Qui d'un courage au mal exercité
Soustint le choc de la commune envie,

Tant que sa nef par tant d'ondes ravie
Eut contre soy tout le monde incité,
On n'a point veu le roc d'adversité
Rompre sa course heureusement suivie.

Mais defaillant l'object de sa vertu,
Son pouvoir s'est de luymesme abbatu :
Comme celuy que le cruel orage

A longuement gardé de faire abbord,
Si trop grand vent le chasse sur le port,
Dessus le port se void faire naufrage.

———————————◆◆◆———————————

Sonnet 21. Another simile: the 'ship of state' of Rome withstood buffeting
from all other nations — and was smashed on entry to the harbour. Du Bel-
lay's starting point seems to have been Lucan's lines about Pyrrhus and Han-
nibal failing to conquer Rome (*Pharsalia*, I, 24–32):

At nunc semirutis pendent quod moenia tectis
Urbibus Italiae lapsisque ingentia muris
Saxa iacent nulloque domus custode tenentur,
Rarus et antiquis habitator in urbibus errat,
Horrida quod dumis multosque inarata per annos
Hesperia est desuntque manus poscentibus arvis,
Non tu, Pyrrhe ferox, nec tantis cladibus auctor
Poenus erit; nulli penitus descendere ferro
Contigit; alta sedent civilis vulnera dextrae.

~ 21 ~

The same which *Pyrrhus,* and the puissaunce
Of *Afrike* could not tame, that same brave Citie,
Which with stout courage arm'd against mischaunce,
Sustein'd the shocke of common enmitie,
   Long as her ship tost with so manie freakes,
Had all the world in armes against her bent,
Was never seene, that anie fortunes wreakes
Could breake her course begun with brave intent.
   But when the object of her vertue failed,
Her power it selfe against it selfe did arme:
As he that having long in tempest sailed,
Faine would arive, but cannot for the storme,
   If too great winde against the port him drive,
   Doth in the port it selfe his vessell rive.

The translation. Du Bellay's *Mars de Libye* (a phrase borrowed from Lucan, *Pharsalia*, I, 255) suggests Hannibal, whereas Spenser seems to refer more generally to the city of Carthage. *Ondes* (l. 5, 'waves') is rendered as 'freakes', meaning 'vicissitudes'; and *roc* (l. 7) by 'wreakes'. Du Bellay's ll. 9–10 mean, literally, 'when an object for her courage was lacking [i.e. when she no longer had anyone left to defeat], her power defeated itself'. 'Rive' (Spenser, l. 14): 'split apart'.

~ 22 ~

Quand ce brave sejour, honneur du nom Latin,
Qui borna sa grandeur d'Afrique et de la Bize,
De ce peuple qui tient les bords de la Tamize,
Et de celuy qui void esclorre le matin,

Anima contre soy d'un courage mutin
Ses propres nourrissons, sa despouille conquise,
Qu'il avoit par tant d'ans sur tout le monde acquise,
Devint soudainement du monde le butin.

Ainsi, quand du grand Tout la fuite retournee,
Où trente six mil' ans ont sa course bornee,
Rompra des elemens le naturel accord,

Les semences qui sont meres de toutes choses,
Retourneront encor' à leur premier discord,
Au ventre du Chaos eternellement closes.

Sonnet 22. Rome conquered the world, from Africa in the south to the far
north (the *Bize* is the north wind and not, as has been said, Byzantium!), and
from Britain in the west to the nation which sees the dawn. But the booty
which Rome took from the world became, after civil war, the world's booty.
In like manner, the breakdown of the harmony of the world will, in due time,
reduce the elements to their primeval chaos. As in s. 9 and 20, the destruction
of Rome affords a premonition of the end of the world.

Du Bellay's starting point is again Lucan who, noting that Rome's fall was
inevitable, added (*Pharsalia*, I, 72–80):
                    Sic cum compage soluta
Saecula tot mundi suprema coegerit hora,
Antiquum repetens iterum chaos, omnia mixtis
Sidera sideribus concurrent, ignea pontum
Astra petent, tellus extendere litora nolet
Excutietque fretum, fratri contraria Phoebe
Ibit et obliquum bigas agitare per orbem
Indignata diem poscet sibi, totaque discors
Machina divulsi turbabit foedera mundi.

Du Bellay's ll. 9–10 refer to the 'great year', the time taken by the heavenly
bodies to return to the same relative position, 36,000 years according to some:
see Plato's *Timaeus*, 39 D and Plutarch's *On fate*, 569 (in his *Moralia*, translated
by P.H. de Lacy and B. Einarson in the Loeb Classical Library, VII, p. 317 and
note). Du Bellay's friend and fellow Pléiade poet, Pontus de Tyard, wrote
about the great year in *Discours du temps, de l'an et de ses parties*, 1556 (see
Saulnier, pp. 130–131).

~ 22 ~

When that brave honour of the Latine name,
   Which mear'd her rule with *Africa*, and *Byze*,
With *Thames* inhabitants of noble fame,
And they which see the dawning day arize,
   Her nourslings did with mutinous uprore
Harten against her selfe, her conquer'd spoile,
Which she had wonne from all the world afore,
Of all the world was spoyl'd within a while.
   So when the compass course of the universe
In six and thirtie thousand yeares is ronne,
The bands of th'elements shall backe reverse
To their first discord, and be quite undonne:
     The seedes, of which all things at first were bred,
     Shall in great *Chaos* wombe againe be hid.

The translation. 'Mear'd' (l. 2): 'measured'. Spenser's 'of noble fame' (l. 3) is an embellishment (doubtless a patriotic one, as in s. 31). He does not render *eternellement*, l. 14.

~ **23** ~

O que celuy estoit cautement sage,
 Qui conseilloit, pour ne laisser moisir
Ses citoyens en paresseux loisir,
De pardonner aux rampars de Carthage!
     Il prevoyoit que le Romain courage,
Impatient du languissant plaisir,
Par le repos se laisseroit saisir
A la fureur de la civile rage.
     Aussi void-on qu'en un peuple ocieux,
Comme l'humeur en un corps vicieux,
L'ambition facilement s'engendre.
     Ce qui advint, quand l'envieux orgueil
De ne vouloir ny plus grand ny pareil
Rompit l'accord du beaupere et du gendre.

Sonnet 23. Du Bellay picks up the theme of s. 21. A wise Roman counselled his compatriots to preserve Carthage: for Rome, if left in idleness, would be destroyed by ambition and civil war. And this is just what happened when Caesar, refusing to grant that anyone was his superior or even his equal, declared war on his father-in-law Pompey. Again (in l. 10), Du Bellay parallels the body politic and the individual: adversity may be useful to the individual as well as the state.

Du Bellay's shrewd Roman is Scipio Nasica Corculum (son-in-law of Scipio Africanus) who, unlike Cato who continually called for the destruction of Carthage, ended his speeches in the Senate by calling for the preservation of Carthage: see Plutarch's *Life of Marcus Cato*, XXVII and Augustine, *City of God*, I, 30. The anecdote was often invoked by Renaissance writers, for example Petrarch (cited by Saulnier, p. 120), Erasmus (*Apophthegmata*, V, 47) and Innocent Gentillet (*Discours contre Machiavel*, ed. A. D'Andrea and P.D. Stewart, Firenze, 1974, pp. 219–220).

~ **23** ~

O warie wisedome of the man, that would
That *Carthage* towres from spoile should be forborne,
To th'end that his victorious people should
With cancring laisure not be overworne!

He well foresaw, how that the Romane courage,
Impatient of pleasures faint desires,
Through idlenes would turne to civill rage,
And be her selfe the matter of her fires.

For in a people given all to ease,
Ambition is engendred easily,
As in a vicious bodie, grose disease
Soone growes through humours superfluitie.

That came to passe, when swolne with plenties pride,
Nor prince, nor peere, nor kin they would abide.

The translation. Spenser's 'cancring' (l. 4) is an elaboration on Du Bellay's *paresseux* ('lazy'). His last two lines (corresponding to Du Bellay's last three) depart substantially from the original. Du Bellay's *envieux orgueil* (l. 12) means 'hate-filled [or 'envious'] pride'; more especially, his 'father-in-law' and 'son-in-law' (l. 14) are patently Pompey and Caesar, an allusion which seems to have escaped Spenser (and will again escape him in s. 31).

~ 24 ~

Si l'aveugle fureur, qui cause les batailles,
Des pareilz animaux n'a les cœurs allumez,
Soient ceulx qui vont courant ou soient les emplumez,
Ceulx-là qui vont rampant ou les armez d'escailles :
 Quelle ardente Erinnys, de ses rouges tenailles,
Vous pinsetoit les cœurs de rage envenimez,
Quand si cruellement l'un sur l'autre animez
Vous destrempiez le fer en voz propres entrailles ?
 Estoit-ce point, Romains, vostre cruel destin,
Ou quelque vieil peché qui d'un discord mutin
Exerçoit contre vous sa vengeance eternelle —
 Ne permettant des Dieux le juste jugement,
Voz murs ensanglantez par la main fraternelle
Se pouvoir asseurer d'un ferme fondement ?

Sonnet 24. Animals (Du Bellay observes) do not attack those of their own species (a commonplace: see Erasmus's *Adagia*, IV, i, 1, 'Dulce bellum inexpertis') — so why did the Romans turn the sword against themselves? Could it be (he asks) that the civil wars were a divine punishment for that fratricidal act which, at the dawn of Rome's history, blemished the very construction of the city's walls? He is alluding to the legend that Romulus slew Remus in anger after Remus jumped over the walls which he, Romulus, had built round Rome.

The main source of this sonnet is probably Horace's *Epode VII*, which notes that animals do not fight against their own species and sees civil war as a retribution for the slaying of Remus (as Romans often did: see P. Jal, *La guerre civile à Rome*, pp. 406–411). Individual elements in this sonnet echo other authors. Line 8 recalls one of the most famous lines of the *Aeneid* — 'Neu patriae validas in viscera vertite viris' (VI, 833). And l. 13 follows Lucan — 'fraterno primi maduerunt sanguine muri' (*Pharsalia*, I, 95).

French writers were to deplore their own civil wars in terms reminiscent of the quatrains of this sonnet: Ronsard, for example, in the *Remonstrance au peuple de France* of 1562 (in my edition of the *Discours des miseres*, Genève, 1979, p. 129, where analogous passages in other authors are cited – and see Jacques Béreau, *Les églogues*, ed. M. Gautier, Paris, Genève, 1976, p. 177; Pierre de Brach, *Les Poëmes*, Bourdeaux, 1576, B.L. 11475 f 5, 104vo–105ro; Florimond de Raemond, *Histoire de l'heresie*, 2 v., Paris, 1605, B.L. 860 1 8, I, 195vo).

~ 24 ~

If the blinde furie, which warres breedeth oft,
Wonts not t'enrage the hearts of equall beasts,
Whether they fare on foote, or flie aloft,
Or armed be with clawes, or scalie creasts:
    What fell *Erynnis* with hot burning tongs,
Did grype your hearts, with noysome rage imbew'd,
That each to other working cruell wrongs,
Your blades in your owne bowels you embrew'd?
    Was this (ye *Romanes*) your hard destinie?
Or some old sinne, whose unappeased guilt
Powr'd vengeance forth on you eternallie?
Or brothers blood, the which at first was spilt
    Upon your walls, that God might not endure,
    Upon the same to set foundation sure?

The translation. Du Bellay's *pareilz animaux* (animals of the same species) is rendered, rather unclearly, as 'equall beasts'. In l. 5, *ardente* applies in the original to *Erinnys*. *Destrempiez* (l. 8: 'soaked') is rendered as 'embrew'd' ('stained'). *D'un discord mutin* (l. 10: 'with mutinous discord') has no equivalent in Spenser. Spenser's 'Or' in l. 12 distorts Du Bellay's sense: the 'old sin' to which Du Bellay refers is, precisely, the murder of Remus, and a translation of the second tercet (obscurely rendered by Spenser) would be, 'For the just judgement of the gods did not permit that those walls which had been stained with the blood of a brother should be built on a firm foundation'.

~ **25** ~

Que n'ay-je encor la harpe Thracienne,
 Pour réveiller de l'enfer paresseux
Ces vieux Cesars, et les Umbres de ceux
Qui ont basty ceste ville ancienne!

   Ou que je n'ay celle Amphionienne,
Pour animer d'un accord plus heureux
De ces vieux murs les ossemens pierreux,
Et restaurer la gloire Ausonienne!

   Peusse-je aumoins d'un pinceau plus agile
Sur le patron de quelque grand Virgile
De ces palais les protraits façonner:

   J'entreprendrois, veu l'ardeur qui m'allume,
De rebastir au compas de la plume
Ce que les mains ne peuvent maçonner.

Sonnet 25. Du Bellay desires the skill to rebuild ancient Rome — the skill of Orpheus, the legendary Thracian poet and musician who was allowed to bring his wife Eurydice out of the underworld (ll. 1–4), and that of Amphion, who by the power of his music made the stones move and built the ramparts of Thebes (ll. 5–8); or at least the skill of Virgil (ll. 9–11). Orpheus and Amphion enjoyed higher prestige than Virgil as being the ultimate examples of divinely-inspired poets who worked miracles. They were cited together by Horace in his *Ars poetica* (ll. 391–407), and frequently in the Renaissance (for example by Louis Le Caron in his *Dialogues* of 1556: see the edition by J.A. Buhlmann and D. Gilman, Genève, 1986, pp. 261–262 and n. 7).

   As well as comparing poetry here to music, Du Bellay compares it to painting, as in the dedicatory poem *Au Roy* (see the notes to that sonnet), and to architecture, as in his *Regrets* (s. 157 and 158) and in a letter to a friend, Jean Morel (see *Œuvres poétiques*, ed. Chamard, VI, pp. 98–99).

~ 25 ~

O that I had the *Thracian* Poets harpe,
For to awake out of th'infernall shade
Those antique *Cæsars*, sleeping long in darke,
The which this auncient Citie whilome made!
　　Or that I had *Amphions* instrument,
To quicken with his vitall notes accord
The stonie joynts of these old walls now rent,
By which th'*Ausonian* light might be restor'd!
　　Or that at least I could with pencill fine
Fashion the pourtraicts of these Palacis
By paterne of great *Virgils* spirit divine:
I would assay with that which in me is,
　　To builde with levell of my loftie style,
　　That which no hands can evermore compyle.

The translation. Du Bellay seeks to awaken the shades of the Caesars and the builders of Rome; Spenser is content to awaken the emperors (ll. 1–4). The *ardeur* Du Bellay enjoys (l. 12) is poetic inspiration; it is conveyed by 'spirit divine' (l. 11, where it is attributed to Virgil). In l. 13 Du Bellay suggests his pen could become a compass to help him design a new Rome.

~ 26 ~

Qui voudroit figurer la Romaine grandeur
En ses dimensions, il ne luy faudroit querre
A la ligne et au plomb, au compas, à l'equerre,
Sa longueur et largeur, hautesse et profondeur:
    Il luy faudroit cerner d'une egale rondeur
Tout ce que l'Ocean de ses longs bras enserre,
Soit ou l'Astre annuel eschauffe plus la terre,
Soit ou souffle Aquilon sa plus grande froideur.
    Rome fut tout le monde, et tout le monde est Rome.
Et si par mesmes noms mesmes choses on nomme,
Comme du nom de Rome on se pourroit passer
    La nommant par le nom de la terre et de l'onde,
Ainsi le monde on peult sur Rome compasser,
Puisque le plan de Rome est la carte du monde.

Sonnet 26. Man-made instruments cannot measure Rome (ll. 1–4), which is synonymous with everything that Ocean embraces in its long arms, from the Equator to the poles (ll. 5–8). You measure the greatness of Rome by measuring the world, and a fitting name for Rome is 'world' (ll. 9–14): Du Bellay repeats the key concepts *Rome, monde* and *nom*.

In l. 9, the chiasmus underlines the contrast between the past and present verbs. But how can Du Bellay say, as he does here, that the ruined city of Rome still holds universal sway? Roman power (he has told us in s. 8, 17 and 18) has been transferred from politics to religion: he is alluding here to the universal (that is, 'catholic') Church.

~ 26 ~

Who list the Romane greatnes forth to figure,
Him needeth not to seeke for usage right
Of line, or lead, or rule, or squaire, to measure
Her length, her breadth, her deepnes, or her hight:
　　But him behooves to vew in compasse round
All that the Ocean graspes in his long armes,
Be it where the yerely starre doth scortch the ground,
Or where colde *Boreas* blowes his bitter stormes.
　　Rome was th'whole world, and al the world was *Rome*,
And if things nam'd their names doo equalize,
When land and sea ye name, then name ye *Rome*,
And naming *Rome* ye land and sea comprize:
　　For th'auncient Plot of *Rome* displayed plaine,
　　The map of all the wide world doth containe.

The translation. Spenser significantly alters l. 9 by keeping the verb in the past, thus negating the notion that Rome is still synonymous with the world. Similarly, he uses a past tense of the verb in the conclusion to the sonnet. The effect of his alterations is to remove all suggestion that Rome has any present status (let alone the universal authority suggested by Du Bellay).

~ 27 ~

Toy qui de Rome emerveillé contemples
L'antique orgueil, qui menassoit les cieux,
Ces vieux palais, ces monts audacieux,
Ces murs, ces arcz, ces thermes et ces temples :
    Juge, en voyant ces ruines si amples,
Ce qu'a rongé le temps injurieux,
Puis qu'aux ouvriers les plus industrieux
Ces vieux fragmens encor servent d'exemples.
    Regarde apres, comme de jour en jour
Rome fouillant son antique sejour
Se rebatist de tant d'œuvres divines :
    Tu jugeras que le dæmon Romain
S'efforce encor d'une fatale main
Ressusciter ces poudreuses ruines.

Sonnet 27. To this day, the mere rubble of Rome affords models for the best artisans — and as modern buildings are based on those of ancient times, you would say that the spirit of Rome is striving to this day to restore the city. As in s. 3, Du Bellay invites the reader to place himself amidst the ruins, and reflect. The architecture of the sonnet underlines the invitations to observe (l. 1, l. 9) and then to judge (l. 5, l. 12).

~ **27** ~

Thou that at *Rome* astonisht dost behold
   The antique pride, which menaced the skie,
These haughtie heapes, these palaces of olde,
These wals, these arcks, these baths, these temples hie:
      Judge by these ample ruines vew, the rest,
The which injurious time hath quite outworne,
Since of all workmen helde in reckning best,
Yet these olde fragments are for paternes borne.
      Then also marke, how Rome from day to day,
Repayring her decayed fashion,
Renewes herselfe with buildings rich and gay:
That one would judge, that the *Romaine Dæmon*
      Doth yet himselfe with fatall hand enforce,
      Againe on foote to reare her pouldred corse.

The translation. Du Bellay's *industrieux* (l. 7) ('diligent') is rendered as 'helde in reckning best'. His ll. 9–14 mean, literally, 'Observe next how Rome, rifling day by day her ancient abode, is reconstructing herself with all these divine works. You will judge that the spirit of Rome is striving, with a hand guided by Fate, to resurrect these dusty ruins'. Spenser's 'pouldred corse' means 'powdered [i.e. pulverized] corpse'.

~ 28 ~

Qui a veu quelquefois un grand chesne asseiché,
Qui pour son ornement quelque trophee porte,
Lever encor' au ciel sa vieille teste morte,
Dont le pied fermement n'est en terre fiché,

Mais qui dessus le champ plus qu'à demy panché
Monstre ses bras tous nuds et sa racine torte,
Et sans fueille umbrageux, de son poix se supporte
Sur son tronc noüailleux en cent lieux esbranché,

Et bien qu'au premier vent il doive sa ruine,
Et maint jeune à l'entour ait ferme la racine,
Du devot populaire estre seul reveré :

Qui tel chesne a peu voir, qu'il imagine encores
Comme entre les cités, qui plus florissent ores
Ce vieil honneur poudreux est le plus honnoré.

Sonnet 28. A great oak tree, though dead, is admired more than healthy saplings — and that is the relation of Rome to other cities. For even today, Rome, though reduced to rubble, is the most revered of cities.

Du Bellay's source is Lucan's verdict on Pompey (*Pharsalia*, I, 135–143):

Stat, magni nominis umbra,
Qualis frugifero quercus sublimis in agro
Exuvias veteris populi sacrataque gestans
Dona ducum; nec iam validis radicibus haeret,
Pondere fixa suo est, nudosque per aera ramos
Effundens, trunco non frondibus efficit umbram;
Sed quamvis primo nutet casura sub Euro,
Tot circum silvae firmo se robore tollant,
Sola tamen colitur.

The oak is traditionally associated with strength (see, for example, Alciati, *Emblemata*, 42, 199). It is also the tree of Jupiter (the responses of the oracle in the sanctuary of Zeus at Dodona came from a sacred oak). Hence, the oak is revered by the pious (l. 11): as elsewhere, Du Bellay alludes to the sacred status of Rome.

~ 28 ~

He that hath seene a great Oke drie and dead,
  Yet clad with reliques of some Trophees olde,
Lifting to heaven her aged hoarie head,
Whose foote in ground hath left but feeble holde,
    But halfe disbowel'd lies above the ground,
Shewing her wreathed rootes, and naked armes,
And on her trunke all rotten and unsound
Onely supports herselle for meate of wormes,
    And though she owe her fall to the first winde,
Yet of the devout people is ador'd,
And manie yong plants spring out of her rinde:
Who such an Oke hath seene, let him record
    That such this Cities honour was of yore,
    And mongst all Cities florished much more.

The translation. Spenser's 'hoary' does not convey Du Bellay's 'dead' tree (l. 3). *Panché* (l. 5) means 'leaning', i.e. the oak was tilted more than halfway to the ground. Du Bellay's ll. 7–8 mean 'And with no shady leaves, stays upright with its own weight, upon a knotty trunk which in a hundred places has been stripped of branches'. Du Bellay's l. 10 means 'and many a young one [a young oak] round about it is firmly rooted'. But Spenser's most significant alteration by far is to Du Bellay's conclusion, which reads: 'Let anyone who has seen such an oak go on to reflect how, among the most flourishing cities of today, this old city, reduced to rubble, is honourable — and is the city which is honoured most'. Du Bellay's reference in l. 11 to pious people venerating Rome, and his use of the present tense in his conclusion, and his remarks in other sonnets about the continuing authority of Rome — all that suggests Du Bellay was thinking here of the religious jurisdiction of Rome. Spenser rewrote the sonnet to place esteem for Rome in the past. 'This poem shows translation blending into critical reinterpretation as du Bellay's images of both ancient Rome and her modern heirs are filtered through a Protestant lens' (Ferguson in *The Spenser encyclopedia*, p. 186).

~ 29 ~

Tout ce qu'Egypte en poincte façonna,
  Tout ce que Græce à la Corinthienne,
A l'Ionique, Attique ou Dorienne,
Pour l'ornement des temples maçonna ;
  Tout ce que l'art de Lysippe donna,
La main d'Apelle ou la main Phidienne,
Souloit orner ceste ville ancienne,
Dont la grandeur le ciel mesme estonna ;
  Tout ce qu'Athene' eut onques de sagesse,
Tout ce qu'Asie eut onques de richesse,
Tout ce qu'Afrique eut onques de nouveau
  S'est veu icy. O merveille profonde !
Rome vivant fut l'ornement du monde,
Et morte elle est du monde le tumbeau.

──────────◆◆◆──────────

Sonnet 29. Rome was the centre of all the culture and wealth of mankind (Lysippus and Phidias were Greek sculptors and Apelles was a Greek painter). While Rome lived, she embellished the world, and now that she is dead she is the tomb of the world. Once again, Rome is the universal city, emblematic of mankind; again, the sonnet suggests hubris and its punishment, for the soaring obelisks, temples and statues challenge the gods (l. 8) — and are consigned to the grave (l. 14).

The architecture of the sonnet projects the content: the repetitions ('Tout ce que') place the emphasis on the last lines where the thrust of the sonnet is found; the conclusion is further stressed by the antithesis between l. 13 and l. 14, and by the concluding word *tombeau*, 'tomb', a *leitmotif* of the collection.

~ 29 ~

All that which *Aegypt* whilome did devise,
All that which *Greece* their temples to embrave,
After th'Ionicke, Atticke, Doricke guise,
Or *Corinth* skil'd in curious workes to grave;
    All that *Lysippus* practike arte could forme,
Apelles wit, or *Phidias* his skill,
Was wont this auncient Citie to adorne,
And the heaven it selfe with her wide wonders fill;
    All that which *Athens* ever brought forth wise,
All that which *Afrike* ever brought forth strange,
All that which *Asie* ever had of prise,
Was here to see. O mervelous great change!
    Rome living, was the worlds sole ornament,
    And dead, is now the worlds sole moniment.

The translation. Spenser omits the specific reference (l. 1) to the Egyptian obelisks; 'wit' and 'skill' (l. 6) are embellishments on *main*. In l. 8, Spenser makes the works of art, rather than the greatness of Rome, the subject of the verb. Spenser's l. 12, with the reference (not in Du Bellay) to 'change', anticipates the conclusion; and in his last line, 'moniment' is less dramatic than Du Bellay's *tombeau*.

~ 30 ~

Comme le champ semé en verdure foisonne,
De verdure se haulse en tuyau verdissant,
Du tuyau se herisse en epic florissant,
D'epic jaunit en grain, que le chaud assaisonne ;
  Et comme en la saison le rustique moissonne
Les ondoyans cheveux du sillon blondissant,
Les met d'ordre en javelle, et du blé jaunissant
Sur le champ despouillé mille gerbes façonne :
  Ainsi de peu à peu creut l'empire Romain,
Tant qu'il fut despouillé par la Barbare main,
Qui ne laissa de luy que ces marques antiques,
  Que chacun va pillant — comme on void le gleneur
Cheminant pas à pas recueillir les reliques
De ce qui va tumbant apres le moissonneur.

Sonnet 30. Rome was like a field of wheat which, when ripe, was harvested by the barbarians — who left us just the ruins, as a harvester leaves a few ears of corn for the gleaners. The sonnet seems to have two messages: that human perfection, like a ripe harvest, is but momentary (Du Bellay is perhaps echoing *Mark*, IV, 28–29); and that recent societies are mere 'crumbs' of the civilization that was Rome (the 'gleaner's share', proverbially, is a fragment of the harvest: see the book of *Ruth*, II).

~ 30 ~

L ike as the seeded field greene grasse first showes,
Then from greene grasse into a stalke doth spring,
And from a stalke into an eare forth-growes,
Which eare the frutefull graine doth shortly bring;
    And as in season due the husband mowes
The waving lockes of those faire yeallow heares,
Which bound in sheaves, and layd in comely rowes,
Upon the naked fields in stackes he reares:
    So grew the Romane Empire by degree,
Till that Barbarian hands it quite did spill,
And left of it but these olde markes to see,
Of which all passers by doo somewhat pill —
    As they which gleane, the reliques use to gather,
    Which th'husbandman behind him chanst to scater.

The translation. In l. 4, Du Bellay says 'and the warmth gives a good flavour to it'; Spenser does not render this. Du Bellay's l. 6 means, literally, 'the curly hair of the yellowing furrow'. Spenser's 'heares' (l. 6) are 'hairs'. The point of Du Bellay's *mille gerbes* (l. 8), not rendered by Spenser, is that there are a thousand sheaves, i.e. a great number (to be contrasted with the meagre ears of corn which fall to the 'gleaners', that is to subsequent generations). Spenser does not render *Cheminant pas à pas* (l. 13: 'proceeding step by step'), though the loss is not great.

~ 31 ~

De ce qu'on ne void plus qu'une vague campaigne,
Où tout l'orgueil du monde on a veu quelquefois,
Tu n'en es pas coulpable, ô quiconques tu sois
Que le Tygre et le Nil, Gange et Euphrate baigne.

Coulpables n'en sont pas l'Afrique ni l'Espaigne,
Ny ce peuple qui tient les rivages Anglois,
Ni ce brave soldat qui boit le Rhin Gaulois,
Ni cest autre guerrier, nourrisson d'Alemaigne.

Tu en es seule cause, ô civile fureur,
Qui semant par les champs l'Emathienne horreur,
Armas le propre gendre encontre son beaupere :

Afin qu'estant venue à son degré plus hault,
La Romaine grandeur, trop longuement prospere,
Se vist ruer à bas d'un plus horrible sault.

***

Sonnet 31. A survey of the foes of Rome — none of whom is responsible for the fall of Rome: the responsibility lies with the *bella per Emathios plus quam civilia campos* (Lucan, *Pharsalia*, I, 1, echoed in ll. 9–10), the civil wars in the Emathian fields.

The alternation of ten-syllable and twelve-syllable lines ceases here. In the original edition two sonnets were printed on each page, with the sonnet in decasyllabic lines above: in these last two sonnets, the order is inverted, perhaps to emphasise the conclusion to the work (see the article by Fontaine).

~ 31 ~

That same is now nought but a champian wide,
Where all this worlds pride once was situate.
No blame to thee, whosoever dost abide
By *Nyle*, or *Gange*, or *Tygre*, or *Euphrate*.
    Ne *Afrike* thereof guiltie is, nor *Spaine*,
Nor the bolde people by the *Thamis* brincks,
Nor the brave warlicke brood of *Alemaine*,
Nor the borne Souldier which *Rhine* running drinks.
    Thou onely cause, 0 Civill furie, art
Which sowing in th'*Aemathian* fields thy spight,
Didst arme thy hand against thy proper hart:
To th'end that when thou wast in greatest hight
    To greatnes growne, through long prosperitie,
    Thou then adowne might'st fall more horriblie.

The translation. Du Bellay's *vague campagne* (l. 1) means 'an empty expanse' (as does Spenser's 'champian'). Spenser's 'bolde' (l. 6) is an embellishment (no doubt a patriotic one, as in s. 22); and he omits, in l. 8, Du Bellay's claim (in his l. 8) that the Rhine is 'Gallic'. L. 11 in Du Bellay says 'you armed the very son-in-law against his father-in-law', referring to Caesar and Pompey, an allusion which Spenser omits (as he did in his rendering of s. 23). Du Bellay's second tercet seems to me to be separate from the invocation to civil war in the preceding lines; Spenser takes a different view, but with confusing results (his l. 9 is addressed to 'Civill furie', and l. 12 seems as though it ought to be addressed to Rome).

~ **32** ~

Esperez vous que la posterité
Doive, mes vers, pour tout jamais vous lire ?
Esperez vous que l'œuvre d'une lyre
Puisse acquerir telle immortalité ?

    Si sous le ciel fust quelque eternité,
Les monumens que je vous ai fait dire,
Non en papier, mais en marbre et porphyre,
Eussent gardé leur vive antiquité.

    Ne laisse pas toutefois de sonner,
Luth, qu'Apollon m'a bien daigné donner :
Car si le temps ta gloire ne desrobbe,

    Vanter te peux, quelque bas que tu sois,
D'avoir chanté, le premier des François,
L'antique honneur du peuple à longue robbe.

Sonnet 32. Will these poems be immortal? If immortality existed, the monuments of Rome, which are made of marble, not paper, would have been preserved. But these poems (if they live) can claim to be the first French monument to Rome.

~ 32 ~

Hope ye my verses that posteritie
Of age ensuing shall you ever read?
Hope ye that ever immortalitie
So meane Harpes worke may chalenge for her meed?
    If under heaven anie endurance were,
These moniments, which not in paper writ,
But in Porphyre and Marble doo appeare,
Might well have hop'd to have obtained it.
    Nath'les my Lute, whom *Phœbus* deignd to give,
Cease not to sound these olde antiquities:
For if that time doo let thy glorie live,
Well maist thou boast, how ever base thou bee,
    That thou art first, which of thy Nation song
    Th'olde honour of the people gowned long.

The translation. Du Bellay's ll. 3–4 mean 'Do you hope that the work of a lyre can acquire such immortality?' Spenser's 'meed', l. 4, means 'reward'. There is no equivalent in the original for Spenser's 'these olde antiquities' (l. 10).

~ *L'Envoy* ~

Bellay, first garland of free Poësie
That *France* brought forth, though fruitfull of brave wits,
Well worthie thou of immortalitie,
That long hast traveld by thy learned writs,
   Olde *Rome* out of her ashes to revive,
And give a second life to dead decayes:
Needes must he all eternitie survive,
That can to other give eternall dayes.
   Thy dayes therefore are endles, and thy prayse
Excelling all, that ever went before;
And after thee, gins *Bartas* hie to rayse
His heavenly Muse, th'Almightie to adore.
   Live happie spirits, th'honour of your name,
   And fill the world with never dying fame.

L'envoy. Spenser points to Du Bellay and Guillaume de Salluste (*sieur* Du Bartas) as the two greatest French poets — the latter for either his *Uranie* (1574) or his biblical epic, *La sepmaine de la creation du monde* (1578) and *La seconde sepmaine* (1584); English translations of Du Bartas by Joshua Sylvester appeared between 1590 and 1614 (see S. Snyder, 'Du Bartas, Guillaume de Salluste', in *The Spenser encyclopedia*, p. 80). The absence of Ronsard from this tribute to French poetry is astonishing, especially as Spenser knew his work (see A.L. Prescott, 'French Renaissance literature' in *The Spenser encyclopedia*, pp. 320–321). The likely explanation (bearing in mind Spenser's expurgation of Du Bellay's Roman Catholicism) is that Ronsard was a famous defender of the Catholic faith (see my edition of his *Discours des miseres*, pp. 23–24).

Songe ou Vision (1558)

Visions of Bellay (1591)

~ 1 ~

C'estoit alors que le present des Dieux
  Plus doulcement s'écoule aux yeux de l'homme,
Faisant noyer dedans l'oubly du somme
Tout le soucy du jour laborieux,

    Quand un Dæmon apparut à mes yeux
Dessus le bord du grand fleuve de Rome,
Qui m'appellant du nom dont je me nomme,
Me commanda regarder vers les cieux :

    Puis m'escria : Voy (dit-il) et contemple
Tout ce qui est compris sous ce grand temple,
Voy comme tout n'est rien que vanité.

    Lors cognoissant la mondaine inconstance,
Puis que Dieu seul au temps fait resistance,
N'espere rien qu'en la divinité.

Sonnet 1. The setting is Rome (l. 6) — which in this collection, as in the *Antiquitez,* is representative of the whole world. A spirit appears to Du Bellay and exhorts him to 'see and reflect': as in the *Antiquitez,* the visual is a starting-point for reflection. In this sonnet and throughout the *Songe,* Du Bellay contrasts the divine and the human, the durable and the ephemeral — for everything beneath 'this great temple', the vault of heaven, is but vanity (ll. 10–11).

The theme of vanity and its expression here recalls *Ecclesiastes* (I, 2). French Renaissance poets frequently drew inspiration from this haunting book: see Terence Cave's *Devotional poetry in France c. 1570–1613,* Cambridge, England, 1969, pp. 44–45 (Gabriel Chappuys, translating Diego de Estella); 64 (Rémy Belleau); 98, n. 2 (Jacques Lect); 150 (Antoine de La Roche Chandieu). See also Ronsard's *Elegie à Robert de la Haye* (in his *Œuvres complètes,* ed. Laumonier, X, p. 318).

~ 1 ~

It was the time, when rest soft sliding downe
From heavens hight into mens heavy eyes,
In the forgetfulnes of sleepe doth drowne
The carefull thoughts of mortall miseries:
    Then did a Ghost before mine eyes appeare,
On that great rivers banck, that runnes by Rome,
Which calling me by name, bad me to reare
My lookes to heaven whence all good gifts do come,
    And crying lowd, loe now beholde (quoth he)
What under this great temple placed is:
Lo all is nought but flying vanitee.
So I that know this worlds inconstancies,
    Sith onely God surmounts all times decay,
    In God alone my confidence do stay.

The translation. Spenser's 'whence all good gifts do come' (l. 8) has no equivalent in Du Bellay. In l. 9, he conveys Du Bellay's *Voy* ('beholde') but not *et contemple*, thus omitting the suggestion that observation leads to reflection. The most significant alteration is in ll. 12–14: Du Bellay offers an exhortation to the reader, Spenser describes his own state of mind (or that of the spirit which had appeared to him: his wording is ambivalent).

As in the *Antiquitez,* Du Bellay alternates twelve-syllable and ten-syllable lines; Spenser's translations, as in the *Ruines,* are all decasyllabic.

~ 2 ~

Sur la croppe d'un mont je vis une Fabrique
De cent brasses de hault : cent columnes d'un rond
Toutes de diamant ornoient le brave front,
Et la façon de l'œuvre estoit à la Dorique.

La muraille n'estoit de marbre ny de brique,
Mais d'un luisant crystal, qui du sommet au fond
Elançoit mille raiz de son ventre profond
Sur cent degrez dorez du plus fin or d'Afrique.

D'or estoit le lambriz, et le sommet encor
Reluisoit escaillé de grandes lames d'or :
Le pavé fut de jaspe et d'esmeraulde fine.

O vanité du monde ! Un soudain tremblement
Faisant crouler du mont la plus basse racine,
Renversa ce beau lieu depuis le fondement.

Sonnet 2. A fabulous, towering building comes crashing down. In several sonnets of the *Antiquitez,* Du Bellay had evoked structures which soar towards heaven — obelisks, temples, statues — and hinted that they symbolized hubris (and were analogous to the mountains piled on top of each other by the Giants in their bid to scale heaven). Here and elsewhere in the *Songe* (s. 3, 4, 5, 7, 11), Du Bellay presents exotic or splendid objects or creatures which soar towards heaven and are instantaneously brought low. The allusion to vanity in l. 12 links this sonnet with the preceding one and provides the key to its meaning: Du Bellay is orientating the reader's reflection. According to Gadoffre ('Le message codé [. . .]', pp. 157–158) this sonnet describes the *tempietto* of San Pietro in Montorio on the site of the execution of St. Peter.

~ 2 ~

On high hills top I saw a stately frame,
An hundred cubits high by just assize,
With hundreth pillours fronting faire the same,
All wrought with Diamond after Dorick wise:
Nor brick, nor marble was the wall in view,
But shining Christall, which from top to base
Out of her womb a thousand rayons threw,
One hundred steps of Afrike golds enchase:
Golde was the parget, and the seeling bright
Did shine all scaly with great plates of golde;
The floore of Jasp and Emeraude was dight.
O worlds vainesse. Whiles thus I did behold,
An earthquake shooke the hill from lowest seat,
And overthrew this frame with ruine great.

The translation. *Lambriz* (l. 9): 'ceiling'; *sommet* (l. 9): 'roof' (Spenser's 'parget' means ornamental work in plaster — not a very accurate rendering); 'Whiles thus I did behold' (l. 12) has no equivalent in Du Bellay.

~ 3 ~

Puis m'apparut une Poincte aguisee
D'un diamant de dix piedz en carré,
A sa hauteur justement mesuré,
Tant qu'un archer pourroit prendre visee.

Sur ceste poincte une urne fut posee
De ce metal sur tous plus honnoré:
Et reposoit en ce vase doré
D'un grand Cesar la cendre composee.

Aux quatre coings estoient couchez encor
Pour pedestal quatre grans lyons d'or,
Digne tumbeau d'une si digne cendre.

Las, rien ne dure au monde que torment!
Je vy du ciel la tempeste descendre,
Et foudroyer ce brave monument.

Sonnet 3. An obelisk made of a colossal diamond, as high as the distance an archer can fire an arrow, supports a golden urn containing the ashes of an emperor, with four golden lions at the base — until a lightning flash destroys it. The sonnet appears to refer to the obelisk in the Vatican which had a golden urn at its summit supposedly containing the ashes of Julius Caesar (see Gadoffre, 'Le message codé [...]', pp. 158–160). The moral of the *Antiquitez,* that all human greatness is ephemeral, is reiterated and accentuated: the ashes of an emperor, even, are subject to instant destruction.

~ **3** ~

Then did a sharped spyre of Diamond bright,
Ten feete each way in square, appeare to mee,
Justly proportion'd up unto his hight,
So far as Archer might his level see:
    The top thereof a pot did seeme to beare,
Made of the mettall, which we most do honour,
And in this golden vessell couched weare
The ashes of a mightie Emperour:
    Upon foure corners of the base were pight,
To beare the frame, foure great Lyons of gold;
A worthy tombe for such a worthy wight.
Alas this world doth nought but grievance hold.
    I saw a tempest from the heaven descend,
    Which this brave monument with flash did rend.

The translation. Spenser's rendering is very close to the original. 'Pight' (l. 9): 'set', 'placed'.

~ **4** ~

Je vy hault eslevé sur columnes d'ivoire,
Dont les bases estoient du plus riche metal,
A chapiteaux d'albastre et frizes de crystal,
Le double front d'un arc dressé pour la memoire.

A chaque face estoit protraicte une victoire,
Portant ailes au doz, avec habit nymphal,
Et hault assise y fut sur un char triomphal
Des Empereurs Romains la plus antique gloire.

L'ouvrage ne monstroit un artifice humain,
Mais sembloit estre fait de celle propre main
Qui forge en aguisant la paternelle foudre.

Las, je ne veulx plus voir rien de beau sous les cieux,
Puis qu'un œuvre si beau j'ay veu devant mes yeux
D'une soudaine cheute estre reduict en poudre.

Sonnet 4. A triumphal arch bears a chariot containing the most illustrious of emperors. This superhuman structure appears to be the work of Vulcan (ll. 10–11) — but in a sudden fall is reduced to rubble. Vulcan was (among other things) the god of alchemists: Heather Ingman has pointed to the use in the *Songe* of the language of alchemy. According to Gadoffre ('Le message codé [...]', pp. 160–163), this sonnet describes the twin arch known as *Janus quadrifons*, Janus being a god who was habitually shown (like St. Peter) as bearing a key; thus, Du Bellay may be alluding to the ruin of an edifice associated with the papacy.

~ 4 ~

I saw raysde up on yvorie pilloures tall,
Whose bases were of richest mettalls warke,
The chapters Alablaster, the fryses christall,
The double front of a triumphall Arke:
    On each side purtraid was a Victorie,
Clad like a Nimph, that wings of silver weares,
And in triumphant chayre was set on hie,
The auncient glory of the Romaine Peares.
    No work it seem'd of earthly craftsmans wit,
But rather wrought by his owne industry,
That thunder-dartes for Jove his syre doth fit.
Let me no more see faire thing under sky,
    Sith that mine eyes have seen so faire a sight
    With sodain fall to dust consumed quight.

The translation. Spenser's 'chapters' (l. 4) are capitals. His 'of silver' (l. 6) has no equivalent in Du Bellay, but otherwise his rendering is very close. (The text has 'pillowes' in l. 1, patently a mistake.)

~ 5 ~

Et puis je vy l'Arbre Dodonien
Sur sept costaux espandre son umbrage,
Et les vainqueurs ornez de son fueillage
Dessus le bord du fleuve Ausonien.

   Là fut dressé maint trophee ancien,
Mainte despouille, et maint beau tesmoignage
De la grandeur de ce brave lignage
Qui descendit du sang Dardanien.

   J'estoy ravy de voir chose si rare,
Quand de paisans une troppe barbare
Vint oultrager l'honneur de ces rameaux.

   J'ouy le tronc gemir sous la congnee,
Et vy depuis la souche desdaignee
Se reverdir en deux arbres jumeaux.

Sonnet 5. The *arbre Dodonien* (the oak, for at Dodona oaks were dedicated to Zeus) spreads its foliage over seven hills, and conquerors are bedecked with its foliage beside the river of the Ausones (the ancient inhabitants of Italy); and many an ancient trophy bears witness to the prowess of the descendants of Dardanus (the son of Zeus and Electra, ancestor of the Trojans and hence of the Romans). And then barbarians cut down the oak, and from its trunk two verdant saplings spring.

   For some commentators, the two new trees are the empires of east and west; for others, they are the holy Roman empire and the papacy. An alternative would be that they are the political and religious heirs, as Du Bellay saw it, of ancient Roman authority: the French state (determined to achieve universal dominion — see the dedicatory poem in the *Antiquitez*, note) and the Church of Rome.

~ 5 ~

Then was the fair Dodonian tree far seene,
 Upon seaven hills to spread his gladsome gleame,
And conquerours bedecked with his greene,
Along the bancks of the Ausonian streame:
　There many an auncient Trophee was addrest.
And many a spoyle, and many a goodly show,
Which that brave races greatnes did attest,
That whilome from the Troyan blood did flow.
　Ravisht I was so rare a thing to vew,
When lo a barbarous troupe of clownish fone
The honour of these noble boughs down threw;
Under the wedge I heard the tronck to grone;
　And since I saw the roote in great disdaine
　A twinne of forked trees send forth againe.

The translation. Spenser's 'gladsome gleam' (l. 2) elaborates on Du Bellay's *umbrage* (= 'shade'). 'Fone' (l. 10): 'foes'.

~ 6 ~

Une Louve je vy sous l'antre d'un rocher
Allaictant deux bessons : je vis à sa mamelle
Mignardement joüer ceste couple jumelle,
Et d'un col allongé la Louve les lecher.

Je la vy hors de là sa pasture chercher,
Et courant par les champs, d'une fureur nouvelle
Ensanglanter la dent et la patte cruelle
Sur les menus troppeaux pour sa soif estancher.

Je vy mille veneurs descendre des montagnes
Qui bornent d'un costé les Lombardes campagnes
Et vy de cent espieux luy donner dans le flanc.

Je la vy de son long sur la plaine estendue,
Poussant mille sanglotz, se veautrer en son sang,
Et dessus un vieux tronc la despouille pendue.

Sonnet 6. A she-wolf feeds twins, and kills other animals in the fields —
and then hunters appear from the north and slay her. The allusions are
successively to the she-wolf which (according to legend) saved the infants
Romulus and Remus by feeding them, to Rome's conquests and to Rome's
destruction at the hands of the barbarians. Like most others, this sonnet begins
with the statement *je vy*, 'I saw'; here, the verb recurs several times. Du Bellay
is echoing the presentation of material in the *Apocalypse* or *Revelation*.

The first quatrain is reminiscent of a scene engraved on Aeneas's shield
(*Aeneid*, VIII, 630–634):

Fecerat [Vulcanus] et viridi fetam Mavortis in antro
Procubuisse lupam, geminos huic ubera circum
Ludere pendentis pueros et lambere matrem
Impavidos, illam tereti cervice reflexa
Mulcere alternos et corpora fingere lingua.

~ 6 ~

I saw a Wolfe under a rockie cave
Noursing two whelpes; I saw her litle ones
In wanton dalliance the teate to crave,
While she her neck wreath'd from them for the nones:
    I saw her raunge abroad to seeke her food,
And roming through the field with greedie rage
T'embrew her teeth and clawes with lukewarm blood
Of the small heards, her thirst for to asswage.
    I saw a thousand huntsmen, which descended
Downe from the mountaines bordring Lombardie,
That with an hundred speares her flank wide rended.
I saw her on the plaine outstretched lie,
    Throwing out thousand throbs in her owne soyle:
    Soone on a tree uphang'd I saw her spoyle.

The translation. Du Bellay's *bessons* (l. 2), 'twins', suggests human beings —
in context, the founders of Rome. Du Bellay's l. 4 means 'and with a craning
neck the she-wolf licking them' (Spenser was unable to convey Du Bellay's
sense, let alone his alliteration). Du Bellay's *se veautrer en son sang* (l. 13) means
'wallowing in her blood'.

~ 7 ~

Je vy l'Oyseau, qui le Soleil contemple,
  D'un foible vol au ciel s'avanturer,
Et peu à peu ses ailes asseurer,
Suivant encor le maternel exemple.

  Je le vy croistre, et d'un voler plus ample
Des plus hauts monts la hauteur mesurer,
Percer la nuë, et ses ailes tirer
Jusques au lieu où des Dieux est le temple.

  Là se perdit : puis soudain je l'ay veu
Rouant par l'air en tourbillon de feu,
Tout enflammé sur la plaine descendre.

  Je vy son corps en poudre tout reduit,
Et vy l'oyseau, qui la lumiere fuit
Comme un vermet renaistre de sa cendre.

Sonnet 7. The bird which stares at the sun learns to fly and, gaining strength, flies to the tops of mountains, then disappears into the clouds, soaring towards heaven. This bird is the eagle (the symbol of empire — see G. de Tervarent, *Attributs et symboles dans l'art profane, 1450–1600*, Genève, 1958, col. 4–5). The bird then re-emerges in flames and, crashing to earth, is reduced to dust — whereupon there emerges from its ashes the bird which shuns the light (the owl, the emblem of sleep: see Tervarent, *Attributs et symboles* [. . .], col. 97).

The eagle is obviously Rome, but what does the owl represent? The 'dark ages' which followed the fall of Rome? Or the humble ignorance of the wise man who does not challenge divine authority? Or the Christian Church (Du Bellay had frequently noted in the *Antiquitez* that Rome's universal political supremacy has been replaced by religious jurisdiction)? The owl is traditionally associated with wisdom (see Tervarent, *Attributs* [. . .], col. 96). The light-shunning owl is proverbially the opposite of the eagle: see Erasmus, *Adagia*, I, ix, 18, 'Aquilam noctuæ comparas'.

~ 7 ~

I saw the Bird that can the Sun endure,
With feeble wings assay to mount on hight,
By more and more she gan her wings t'assure,
Following th'ensample of her mothers sight:
    I saw her rise, and with a larger flight
To pierce the cloudes, and with wide pinneons
To measure the most haughtie mountaines hight,
Untill she raught the Gods owne mansions:
    There was she lost, when suddaine I behelde,
Where tumbling through the ayre in firie fold
All flaming downe she on the plaine was felde,
And soone her bodie turn'd to ashes colde.
    I saw the foule that doth the light dispise,
    Out of her dust like to a worme arise.

The translation. Spenser's translation is very close to the original. His 'raught' (l. 8) means 'reached'; 'colde', l. 12, is an embellishment.

~ 8 ~

Je vis un fier Torrent, dont les flots escumeux
 Rongeoient les fondemens d'une vieille ruine :
Je le vy tout couvert d'une obscure bruine,
Qui s'élevoit par l'air en tourbillons fumeux :

  Dont se formoit un corps à sept chefz merveilleux,
Qui villes et chasteaux couvoit sous sa poittrine,
Et sembloit devorer d'une egale rapine
Les plus doulx animaux et les plus orgueilleux.

  J'estois emerveillé de voir ce monstre enorme
Changer en cent façons son effroyable forme,
Lors que je vy sortir d'un antre Scythien

  Ce vent impetueux, qui souffle la froidure,
Dissiper ces nuaux, et en si peu que rien
S'esvanouïr par l'air ceste horrible figure.

Sonnet 8. From the foam thrown up by a raging torrent, a seven-headed monster is formed, and it proceeds to swallow up everything in the world — until the north wind dissipates the monster in an instant. The seven-headed monster suggests simultaneously the Hydra and (perhaps more especially) the seven-headed scarlet beast of *Apocalypse* XIII and XVII, itself a representation of Rome with its seven hills. The north wind represents the invaders who dissipated Rome's power: the Roman empire (even!) is so ephemeral it can be swept away by a breath of wind.

A further explanation suggests itself. The stream (perhaps the 'living water' of the word of Christ — see s. 12) saps the foundations of pagan Rome. But the stream becomes contaminated and spawns the scarlet beast — the wickedness of degenerate papal Rome; and then the corrupt magnificence of the papacy is swept away by the cold wind from the north — the Lutheran revolt. This interpretation is consistent with the historical situation and with later sonnets in this book. Du Bellay (and several other French writers, such as La Boëtie, Ronsard and Montaigne) coupled loyalty to the Church with incisive attacks on corruption.

~ 8 ~

I saw a river swift, whose fomy billowes
Did wash the ground work of an old great wall;
I saw it cover'd all with griesly shadowes,
That with black horror did the ayre appall:
  Thereout a strange beast with seven heads arose,
That townes and castles under her brest did coure,
And seem'd both milder beasts and fiercer foes
Alike with equall ravine to devoure.
  Much was I mazde, to see this monsters kinde
In hundred formes to change his fearefull hew,
When as at length I saw the wrathfull winde,
Which blows cold storms, burst out of Scithian mew
    That sperst these cloudes, and in so short as thought,
    This dreadfull shape was vanished to nought.

The translation. Du Bellay's *bruine* (l. 3) means 'A hot mist that blasteth, and burneth plants' (Cotgrave); he seems to mean that an opaque cloud arose from the stream (Spenser's 'griesly' means 'terrifying', 'ghastly'). Du Bellay's ll. 4–6 mean 'Which rose through the air in whirls of foam, out of which was formed a body with seven amazing heads which, beneath its breast, hatched cities and castles'; Spenser's 'coure' (l. 6): 'cover'. Spenser's 'mew' (l. 12) means a 'den'; his 'sperst' (l. 13) means 'dispersed'.

~ 9 ~

Tout effroyé de ce monstre nocturne,
Je vis un Corps hydeusement nerveux,
A longue barbe, à long flottans cheveux,
A front ridé et face de Saturne :
    Qui s'accoudant sur le ventre d'une urne,
Versoit une eau, dont le cours fluctueux
Alloit baignant tout ce bord sinueux
Où le Troyen combattit contre Turne.
    Dessous ses piedz une Louve allaictoit
Deux enfançons :   sa main dextre portoit
L'arbre de paix, l'autre la palme forte :
    Son chef estoit couronné de laurier.
Adonc luy cheut la palme et l'olivier,
Et du laurier la branche devint morte.

Sonnet 9. A hideously old man (doubtless representing Rome) pours the
River Tiber from an urn while a she-wolf at his feet feeds two young children
(Romulus and Remus). The man bears an olive branch in one hand, a palm in
the other, and a crown of laurel on his head. Suddenly, the palm (a symbol
of victory) and the olive (a symbol of peace) fall from his hand, and the laurel
(a symbol of immortality) dies: Rome's achievements, the greatest known to
man, are set at naught in an instant.

~ 9 ~

Then all astonied with this mighty ghoast,
    An hidous bodie big and strong I sawe,
With side long beard, and locks down hanging loast,
Sterne face, and front full of Saturnlike awe;
    Who leaning on the belly of a pot,
Pourd foorth a water, whose out gushing flood
Ran bathing all the creakie shore aflot,
Whereon the Troyan prince spilt Turnus blood;
    And at his feete a bitch wolfe suck did yeeld
To two young babes: his left the Palme tree stout,
His right hand did the peacefull Olive wield,
And head with Lawrell garnisht was about.
    Sudden both Palme and Olive fell away,
    And faire greene Lawrell branch did quite decay.

The translation. In l. 1, Du Bellay refers to the monster of the previous sonnet as *nocturne*: this is altered by Spenser to 'mightie'. Spenser's 'side long' (l. 3) means 'reaching far down' and 'loast' (also l. 3) means 'loosed'. Du Bellay's *A front ridé* (l. 4) means 'with wrinkled brow'; Spenser's 'awe' (l. 4) is an embellishment, as is his 'spilt Turnus blood' (l. 8, rendering *combattit*), his identification of the tree of l. 11 as the olive and his 'greene' of l. 14. (In l. 1, the 1591 text has 'astoined'; 'astonied', my correction, means 'stunned', 'stupefied'.)

~ 10 ~

Sur la rive d'un fleuve une Nymphe esploree,
Croisant les bras au ciel avec mille sanglotz,
Accordoit ceste plainte au murmure des flotz,
Oultrageant son beau teinct et sa tresse doree :
    Las, où est maintenant ceste face honoree,
Où est ceste grandeur et cest antique los,
Où tout l'heur et l'honneur du monde fut enclos,
Quand des hommes j'estois et des Dieux adoree ?
    N'estoit-ce pas assez que le discord mutin
M'eut fait de tout le monde un publique butin,
Si cest Hydre nouveau, digne de cent Hercules,
    Foisonnant en sept chefz de vices monstrueux,
Ne m'engendroit encor à ces bords tortueux
Tant de cruelz Nerons, et tant de Caligules ?

Sonnet 10. A nymph, representing the city of Rome, evokes her time of glory (ll. 5–8) which has been followed by civil war (l. 9), then by pillage at the hands of the barbarians (l. 10), and now affliction by a new seven-headed Hydra — which requires the attention not of one Hercules but of a hundred, and which is renewing the cruelty of the ancient emperors. The chronological presentation suggests that the sonnet has a topical meaning; and Du Bellay draws a parallel (ll. 11–12) between the Hydra's seven heads and the seven deadly sins. It is possible that the new Hydra is the papacy: in the *Regrets*, Du Bellay compares the task of cleansing the Church to a labour of Hercules (s. 106) and papal Rome to the Hydra (s. 108).

~ 10 ~

Hard by a rivers side a virgin faire,
Folding her armes to heaven with thousand throbs,
And outraging her cheekes and golden haire,
To falling rivers sound thus tun'd her sobs.
  Where is (quoth she) this whilom honoured face?
Where the great glorie and the auncient praise,
In which all worlds felicitie had place,
When Gods and men my honour up did raise?
  Suffis'd it not that civill warres me made
The whole worlds spoile, but that this Hydra new,
Of hundred Hercules to be assaide,
With seven heads, budding monstrous crimes anew,
    So many Neroes and Caligulaes
    Out of these crooked shores must dayly rayse?

The translation. Du Bellay's *l'heur et l'honneur* ('fortune and honour', l. 7) is reduced to 'felicitie' by Spenser. Otherwise the rendering is a close one.

~ 11 ~

Dessus un mont une Flamme allumee
A triple poincte ondoyoit vers les cieux,
Qui de l'encens d'un cedre precieux
Parfumoit l'air d'une odeur embasmee.

D'un blanc oyseau l'aile bien emplumee
Sembloit voler jusqu'au sejour des Dieux,
Et dégoisant un chant melodieux
Montoit au ciel avecques la fumee.

De ce beau feu les rayons escartez
Lançoient par tout mille et mille clartez,
Quand le degout d'une pluie doree

Le vint esteindre. O triste changement!
Ce qui sentoit si bon premierement
Fut corrompu d'une odeur sulphuree.

Sonnet 11. A triple-tipped flame wafts towards heaven, and incense is cast upon it; amid the fragrant flames, a melodiously-singing white bird soars aloft. The flame sheds light everywhere — until it is extinguished by golden raindrops, and the fragrance is corrupted by a sulphurous odour. The flame and the white bird are symbols of the Holy Spirit (in, respectively, *Acts*, II and *Matthew*, III). The theological undertones seem to be strengthened by the *triple pointe* (l. 2), perhaps an allusion to the pope's triple tiara. Thus, the Holy Spirit guided the Church and shed light everywhere (ll. 1–10) — until the flame was extinguished by the golden rain, that is by simony (probably an allusion to the sale of indulgences, the immediate issue which unleashed the Reformation). The sonnet which follows confirms this interpretation — and Du Bellay seems to have analogous messages elsewhere (s. 8, 10, 13 and 14).

~ 11 ~

Upon an hill a bright flame I did see,
  Waving aloft with triple point to skie,
Which like incense of precious Cedar tree,
With balmie odours fil'd th'ayre farre and nie.
  A Bird all white, well feathered on each wing,
Hereout up to the throne of Gods did flie,
And all the way most pleasant notes did sing,
Whilst in the smoake she unto heaven did stie.
  Of this faire fire the scattered rayes forth threw
On everie side a thousand shining beames:
When sudden dropping of a silver dew
(O grievous chance) gan quench those precious flames;
    That it which earst so pleasant sent did yeld,
    Of nothing now but noyous sulphure smeld.

The translation. Spenser's 'like incense' (l. 3) departs from Du Bellay's 'with incense', and his 'farre and wide' (l. 4) is an elaboration. 'Stie' (l. 8): 'rise'. Du Bellay's *pluie dorée*, suggestive of simony, becomes 'silver dew' (l. 11), which seems to miss the point.

~ **12** ~

Je vy sourdre d'un roc une vive Fontaine,
Claire comme crystal aux rayons du Soleil,
Et jaunissant au fond d'un sablon tout pareil
A celuy que Pactol' roule parmy la plaine.

Là sembloit que nature et l'art eussent pris peine
D'assembler en un lieu tous les plaisirs de l'œil :
Et là s'oyoit un bruit incitant au sommeil,
De cent accords plus doulx que ceulx d'une Sirene.

Les sieges et relaiz luisoient d'ivoire blanc,
Et cent Nymphes autour se tenoient flanc à flanc,
Quand des monts plus prochains de Faunes une suyte

En effroyables criz sur le lieu s'assembla,
Qui de ses villains piedz la belle onde troubla,
Mist les sieges par terre et les Nymphes en fuyte.

Sonnet 12. A fountain springs from a rock, and sweet music can be heard and nymphs seen — but the pleasures are swiftly disrupted. Du Bellay here echoes Petrarch's *Rime*, 323, ll. 37–48. This passage of Petrarch, imitated by Marot, had formed the basis for the fourth of the six epigrams from Petrarch/Marot published by Van der Noot in the *Theatre*.

But Du Bellay goes beyond the material in Petrarch to give his sonnet a topical flavour. Petrarch's *chiara fontana* (rendered by Marot simply as 'fontaine d'eau') becomes a *vive fontaine* — doubtless an echo of *John*, IV, 10 (and see s. 8, above). A further addition to Petrarch is the reference to the river Pactolus (l. 4) — which was said to bring down golden sands, and was thus a symbol of great wealth (see Erasmus, *Adagia*, I, vi, 75, 'Pactoli opes'). Thus, the 'living stream' (the word of God) has been corrupted by simony; sensuality reigns, and *nymphes*, that is courtesans, are everywhere. In a further departure from his source, where Petrarch has the earth open and swallow up the scene, Du Bellay has the wealth destroyed by fawns from the neighbouring mountains — doubtless the Lutherans. This sonnet is a sequel to the previous one in which the 'golden rain' of simony extinguishes the flame of the Holy Spirit.

The sonnet again reveals Du Bellay's position on the Reformation. The Reformers scatter the ill-gotten gains of the clerics and disperse the courtesans — but earn no sympathy from Du Bellay: they are fauns (spirits with horns and tails, assimilable to demons), they have a fearful stridency, and they pollute the 'stream' of God's word, introducing false teaching.

~ 12 ~

I saw a spring out of a rocke forth rayle,
As cleare as Christall gainst the Sunnie beames,
The bottome yeallow, like the golden grayle
That bright Pactolus washeth with his streames;
   It seem'd that Art and Nature had assembled
All pleasure there, for which mans hart could long;
And there a noyse alluring sleepe soft trembled,
Of manie accords more sweete than Mermaids song:
   The seates and benches shone as yvorie,
And hundred Nymphes sate side by side about;
When from nigh hills with hideous outcrie,
A troupe of Satyres in the place did rout,
      Which with their villeine feete the streame did ray,
      Threw down the seates, and drove the Nymphs away.

The translation. There is an important nuance in Du Bellay's first quatrain which Spenser does not convey: the stream turns yellow after it has issued from the rock (that is, the pure word of God becomes corrupted by simony). More importantly, Spenser fails to translate Du Bellay's *vive* (l. 1), thus omitting the echo of St. John and, consequently, the invitation to the reader to discern a theological significance. In Du Bellay, ll. 5–6 refer to the pleasures of the eye, and ll. 7–8 to pleasures of the ear: his distinction, much less clear in Spenser, seems designed to project his thought. The Homeric resonance of Du Bellay's *Sirene* (l. 8) is largely lost. Du Bellay's *s'assembla* ('assembled', l. 12) is changed by Spenser. Spenser's 'rayle' (l. 1) means 'flow'; 'grayle' (l. 3): 'gravel'; 'ray' (l. 13): 'defile'.

~ **13** ~

Plus riche assez que ne se monstroit celle
 Qui apparut au triste Florentin,
Jettant ma veüe au rivage Latin,
Je vy de loing surgir une Nasselle :
   Mais tout soudain la tempeste cruelle,
Portant envie à si riche butin,
Vint assaillir d'un Aquilon mutin
La belle Nef des autres la plus belle.
   Finablement l'orage impetueux
Fit abysmer d'un gouphre tortueux
La grand' richesse à nulle autre seconde.
   Je vy sous l'eau perdre le beau thresor,
La belle Nef, et les Nochers encor,
Puis vy la Nef se ressourdre sur l'onde.

Sonnet 13. A ship laden with incredible riches is struck by the north wind, and the vessel and its wealth suddenly sink. Du Bellay is recalling (as he says in l. 2) a vision recorded by Petrarch (*Rime*, 323, ll. 13–24). This passage in Petrarch, as adapted by Marot, formed the basis for the second of the six epigrams included by Van der Noot in his *Theatre*.

But once again, as in the previous sonnet, Du Bellay adds an element not found in his source. The ship resurfaces, without the riches and without the sailors. The ship is a traditional symbol of the Roman Church: St. Peter, the first bishop of Rome, was a fisherman and the Church is metaphorically his boat (as Ronsard also observed, in his *Elégie à Des Autels:* see my edition of his *Discours*, p. 33 and note). Thus, here, when struck by the wind from the north (the Reformation), the ship of Peter sinks — and, cleansed of its greedy clerics, it resurfaces. Du Bellay's criticism of clerical corruption is all the more biting for being veiled. Montaigne, too, compared the Reformation to a storm which gave the Church a salutary buffeting (*Les Essais*, II, xv).

~ **13** ~

Much richer then that vessell seem'd to bee,
Which did to that sad Florentine appeare,
Casting mine eyes farre off, I chaunst to see,
Upon the Latine coast herselfe to reare:
    But suddenly arose a tempest great,
Bearing close envie to these riches rare,
Which gan assaile this ship with dreadfull threat,
This ship, to which none other might compare.
    And finally the storme impetuous
Sunke up these riches, second unto none,
Within the gulfe of greedie Nereus.
I saw both ship and mariners each one,
    And all that treasure drowned in the maine:
    But I the ship saw after raisd' againe.

The translation. Du Bellay's first quatrain means 'Casting my eyes to the Latin shore, I saw approaching in the distance a ship which was wealthier by far than the one which appeared to the melancholic Florentine'; Spenser's syntax here is confusing ('then', l. 1: 'than'). In Du Bellay's second quatrain, an *Aquilon mutin* (a 'mutinous north wind') strikes the vessel — probably an allusion to the northern origin of the Reformation and the fact that it is a revolt against the Church. Spenser refers only to a 'tempest great'. Spenser's 'Nereus' (l. 11; the deity who dwelt at the bottom of the sea) is an embellishment.

~ 14 ~

Ayant tant de malheurs gemy profondement,
Je vis une Cité quasi semblable à celle
Que vid le messager de la bonne nouvelle
Mais basty sur le sable estoit son fondement.

Il sembloit que son chef touchast au firmament,
Et sa forme n'estoit moins superbe que belle :
Digne, s'il en fut onc, digne d'estre immortelle,
Si rien dessous le ciel se fondoit fermement.

J'estois emerveillé de voir si bel ouvrage,
Quand du costé de Nort vint le cruel orage,
Qui soufflant la fureur de son cœur despité

Sur tout ce qui s'oppose encontre sa venüe,
Renversa sur le champ, d'une poudreuse nüe,
Les foibles fondemens de la grande Cité.

Sonnet 14. Du Bellay here sees a city almost resembling the heavenly Jerusalem described in the *Apocalypse* (ch. XXI) — but this city was built on sand. If any earthly achievement were immortal, this would be — but a storm reduced it to rubble. In l. 3, Du Bellay introduces a 'messenger of good news', that is an evangelist: he is referring to St. John who, since the second century A.D., has been identified as the author of the *Apocalypse*.

The edifice which almost resembles the heavenly Jerusalem (ll. 2–3) is, it seems, the worldly Church of the Roman clerics; the statement that it is built on sand echoes Christ's warning that such a city will be washed away (cf. *Matthew* VII, 24–27). Again, the storm comes from the north, and Du Bellay is probably alluding once more to the Lutheran Reformation. And again, the target is the worldliness of the Church rather than its doctrines.

~ 14 ~

L ong having deeply gron'd these visions sad,
I saw a citie like unto that same
Which saw the messenger of tidings glad;
But that on sand was built the goodly frame:
 It seem'd her top the firmament did rayse,
And no lesse rich than faire, right worthie sure
(If ought here worthie) of immortal dayes,
Or if ought under heaven might firme endure.
 Much wondred I to see so faire a wall:
When from the northern coast a storm arose,
Which breathing furie from his inward gall
On all, which did against his course oppose,
 Into a clowde of dust sperst in the aire
 The weake foundations of this Citie faire.

The translation. Du Bellay's *fondement* (l. 4: 'foundation') is loosely rendered by Spenser's 'goodly frame'; and the *superbe* of the original (l. 6) has a moral resonance not conveyed in the translation. Du Bellay's *du costé du Nort* (l. 10) means 'from the northern side' (Spenser seems to have confused *le costé*, 'side' and *la coste,* 'coast'). *Sur le champ* (l. 13) means 'immediately' (this sonnet, like most, describes a sudden vicissitude), which is not conveyed by Spenser.

~ **15** ~

Finablement sur le poinct que Morphee
Plus veritable apparoit à noz yeux
Fasché de voir l'inconstance des cieux
Je voy venir la sœur du grand Typhee :
    Qui bravement d'un morion coiffee
En majesté semblait egale aux Dieux,
Et sur le bord d'un fleuve audacieux
De tout le monde erigeoit un trophee.
    Cent Roys vaincuz gemissoient à ses piedz,
Les bras aux doz honteusement liez :
Lors effroyé de voir telle merveille,
    Le ciel encor je luy voy guerroyer,
Puis tout à coup je la voy foudroyer,
Et du grand bruit en sursault je m'esveille.

Sonnet 15. At the moment when Morpheus, the god of dreams, is most truthful (that is, at dawn: see Saulnier, p. 122), the sister of Typhoeus appears. She has subdued the world and has a hundred vanquished kings at her feet: she then wages war on heaven, and is struck by lightning — and the poet is startled out of sleep.

Typhoeus the Giant was punished for presumption by being struck by lightning by Jupiter. He perhaps represents Charles V, who was denounced as Typhoeus in anti-imperial propaganda, for example a poem by Annibale Caro translated by Du Bellay (see Guy Demerson in *Le Songe à la Renaissance,* p. 174). Who is the sister of Typhoeus? Plausibly Rome: Du Bellay has equated Rome with the Giants several times and this sonnet has echoes of the portrayal of Rome in *Apocalypse* XVII and XVIII.

~ **15** ~

At length, even at the time, when Morpheus
Most trulie doth unto our eyes appeare,
Wearie to see the heavens still wavering thus,
I saw Typhæus sister comming neare;
    Whose head full bravely with a morion hidd,
Did seeme to match the Gods in Majestie.
She by a rivers bancke that swift downe slidd,
Over all the world did raise a Trophee hie;
    An hundred vanquisht Kings under her lay,
With armes bound at their backs in shamefull wize;
Whilst I thus mazed was with great affray,
I saw the heavens in warre against her rize:
        Then downe she stricken fell with clap of thonder,
        That with great noyse I wakte in sudden wonder.

The translation. Spenser does not render the moral connotation of *audacieux*
(l. 7), but otherwise his translation is close. 'Morion' (l. 5): 'helmet'.

Theatre for Worldlings (1569)

~ 1 ~

It was the time when rest the gift of Gods
Sweetely sliding into the eyes of men,
Doth drowne in the forgetfulnesse of slepe,
The carefull travailes of the paineful day:
    Then did a ghost appeare before mine eyes
On that great rivers banke that runnes by Rome,
And calling me then by my propre name,
He bade me upwarde unto heaven looke.
    He cride to me, and loe (quod he) beholde,
What under this great Temple is containde,
Loe all is nought but flying vanitie.
So I knowing the worldes unstedfastnesse,
    Sith onely God surmountes the force of tyme,
    In God alone do stay my confidence.

~ 2 ~

On hill, a frame an hundred cubites hie
I sawe, an hundred pillers eke about,
All of fine Diamant decking the front,
And fashiond were they all in Dorike wise.
    Of bricke, ne yet of marble was the wall,
But shining Christall, which from top to base
Out of deepe vaute threw forth a thousand rayes
Upon an hundred steps of purest golde.
    Golde was the parget: and the sielyng eke
Did shine all scaly with fine golden plates.
The floore was Jaspis, and of Emeraude.
O worldes vanenesse. A sodein earthquake loe,
    Shaking the hill even from the bottome deepe,
    Threwe downe this building to the lowest stone.

~ 3 ~

Then did appeare to me a sharped spire
Of diamant, ten feete eche way in square,
Justly proportionde up unto his height,
So hie as mought an Archer reache with sight.
    Upon the tope therof was set a pot
Made of the mettall that we honour most.
And in this golden vessell couched were
The ashes of a mightie Emperour.
    Upon foure corners of the base there lay
To beare the frame, foure great Lions of golde.
A worthie tombe for such a worthie corps.
Alas, nought in this worlde but griefe endures.
      A sodaine tempest from the heaven, I saw,
      With flushe stroke downe this noble monument.

~ 4 ~

I saw raisde up on pillers of Ivoire,
Whereof the bases were of richest golde,
The chapters Alabaster, Christall frises,
The double front of a triumphal arke.
    On eche side portraide was a victorie.
With golden wings in habite of a Nymph.
And set on hie upon triumphing chaire,
The auncient glorie of the Romane lordes.
    The worke did shewe it selfe not wrought by man,
But rather made by his owne skilfull hande
That forgeth thunder dartes for Jove his sire.
Let me no more see faire thing under heaven,
    Sith I have seene so faire a thing as this,
    With sodaine falling broken all to dust.

~ 5 ~

Then I behelde the fair Dodonian tree,
Upon seven hilles throw forth his gladsome shade,
And Conquerers bedecked with his leaves,
Along the bankes of the Italian streame.
  There many auncient Trophees were erect,
Many a spoile, and many goodly signes,
To shewe the greatnesse of the stately race,
That erst descended form the Trojan bloud.
  Ravisht I was to see so rare a thing,
When barbarous villaines in disordred heape,
Outraged the honour of these noble bowes.
I hearde the tronke to grone under the wedge.
    And since I saw the roote in hie disdaine
    Sende forth againe a twinne of forked trees.

~ 6 ~

I saw the birde that dares heholde the Sunne,
With feeble flight venture to mount to heaven,
By more and more she gan to trust hir wings,
Still folowing th'example of hir damme:
    I saw hir rise, and with a larger flight
Surmount the toppes even of the hiest hilles,
And pierce the cloudes, and with hir wings to reache
The place where is the temple of the Gods.
    There was she lost, and sodenly I saw
Where tombling through the aire in lompe of fire,
All flaming downe she fell upon the plaine.
I saw hir bodie turned all to dust,
    And saw the foule that shunnes the cherefull light
    Out of hir ashes as a worme arise.

~ 7 ~

Then all astonned with this nightly ghost,
  I saw an hideous body big and strong,
Long was his beard, and side did hang his hair,
A grisly forehed and Saturnelike face.
  Leaning against the belly of a pot,
He shed a water, whose outgushing streame
Ran flowing all along the creekie shoare
Where once the Troyan Duke with Turnus fought.
  And at his feete a bitch Wolfe did give sucke
To two yong babes. In his right hand he bare
The tree of peace, in left the conquering Palme,
His head was garnisht with the Laurel bow.
  Then sodenly the Palme and Olive fell,
  And faire greene Laurel witherd up and dide.

~ 8 ~

Hard by a rivers side, a wailing Nimphe,
Folding hir armes with thousand sighs to heaven
Did tune hir plaint to falling rivers sound,
Renting hir faire visage and golden haire,
    Where is (quod she) this whilome honored face?
Where is thy glory and the auncient praise,
Where all [the] worldes hap was reposed,
When erst of Gods and man I worshipt was?
    Alas, suffisde it not that civile bate
Made me the spoile and bootie of the world,
But this new Hydra mete to be assailde
Even by an hundred such as Hercules,
    With seven springing heds of monstrous crimes,
    So many Neroes and Caligulaes
    Must still bring forth to rule this croked shore.

~ 9 ~

Upon a hill I saw a kindled flame,
Mounting like waves with triple point to heaven,
Which of incense of precious Ceder tree
With Balmelike odor did perfume the aire.
A bird all white, well fetherd on hir winges
Hereout did flie up to the throne of Gods,
And singing with most plesant melodie
She climbed up to heaven in the smoke.
Of this faire fire the faire dispersed rayes
Threw forth abrode a thousand shining leames,
When sodain dropping of a golden shoure
Gan quench the glystering flame. O grevous chaunge!
That which erstwhile so pleasaunt scent did yelde,
Of Sulphure now did breathe corrupted smel.

~ **10** ~

I saw a fresh spring rise out of a rocke,
Clere as Christall against the Sunny beames,
The bottome yellow like the shining land,
That golden Pactol drives upon the plaine.
 It seemed that arte and nature strived to joyne
There in one place all pleasures of the eye.
There was to heare a noise alluring slepe
Of many accordes more swete than Mermaids song,
 The seates and benches shone as Ivorie,
An hundred Nymphes sate side by side about,
When from nie hilles a naked rout of Faunes
With hideous cry assembled on the place,
 Which with their feete uncleane the water fouled,
 Threw down the seats, and drove the Nimphs to flight.

~ 11 ~

At length, even at the time when Morpheus
Most truely doth appeare unto our eyes,
Wearie to see th'inconstance of the heavens:
I saw the great Typhæus sister come,
  Hir head full bravely with a morian armed,
In majestie she seemde to matche the Gods.
And on the shore, harde by a violent streame,
She raisde a Trophee over all the worlde.
  An hundred vanquisht kings gronde at hir feete,
Their armes in shamefull wise bounde at their backes.
While I was with so dreadfull sight afrayde,
I saw the heavens warre against hir tho,
  And seing hir striken fall with clap of thunder,
  With so great noyse I start in sodaine wonder.

~ 12 ~

I saw an ugly beast come from the sea,
That seven heads, ten crounes, ten hornes did beare,
Having theron the vile blaspheming name.
The cruell Leopard she resembled much:
    Feete of a beare, a Lions throte she had.
The mightie Dragon gave to hir his power.
One of hir heads yet there I did espie,
Still freshly bleeding of a grievous wounde.
    One cride aloude. What one is like (quod he)
This honoured Dragon, or may him withstande?
And then came from the sea a savage beast,
With Dragons speche, and shewde his force by fire,
    With wondrous signes to make all wights adore
    The beast, in setting of hir image up.

~ 13 ~

I saw a Woman sitting on a beast
Before mine eyes, of Orenge colour hew:
Horror and dreadfull name of blasphemie
Filde hir with pride. And seven heads I saw,
    Ten hornes also the stately beast did beare.
She seemde with glorie of the scarlet faire,
And with fine perle and golde puft up in heart.
The wine of hooredome in a cup she bare.
    The name of Mysterie writ in hir face.
The bloud of Martryrs dere were hir delite.
Most fierce and fell this woman seemde to me.
An Angell then descending downe from Heaven,
    With thondring voice cride out aloude, and sayd,
    Now for a truth great Babylon is fallen.

~ 14 ~

Then might I see upon a white horse set
   The faithfull man with flaming countenaunce,
His head did shine with crounes set therupon.
The worde of God made him a noble name.
   His precious robe I saw embrued with bloud.
Then saw I from the heaven on horses white,
A puissant armie come the selfe same way.
Then cried a shining Angell as me thought,
   That birdes from aire descending downe on earth
Should warre upon the kings, and eate their flesh.
Then did I see the beast and Kings also
Joinying their force to slea the faithfull man.
   But this fierce hatefull beast and all hir traine,
   Is pitilesse throwne downe in pit of fire.

~ 15 ~

I saw new Earth, new Heaven, sayde Saint John.
And loe, the sea (quod he) is now no more.
The holy Citie of the Lorde, from hye
Descendeth garnisht as a loved spouse.
  A voice then sayde, beholde the bright abode
Of God and men. For he shall be their God,
And all their teares he shall wipe cleane away.
Hir brightnesse greater was than can be founde,
  Square was this Citie, and twelve gates it had.
Eche gate was of an orient perfect pearle,
The houses golde, the pavement precious stone.
A lively streame, more cleeere than Christall is,
    Ranne through the mid, sprong from triumphant seat.
    There growes lifes fruite unto the Churches good.

Bibliography

Editions of Du Bellay:

Œuvres poétiques, vols. 1–6 [French works], ed. H. Chamard; vol. 7, 8
[Latin works], ed. Geneviève Demerson (Société des Textes français
modernes), Paris, 1908–1985; revised edition by Y. Bellenger: vol. 1,
Paris, 1982; vol. 3, 4, 5, Paris, 1983.

La Deffence et illustration de la langue françoyse, ed. H. Chamard (Société
des Textes français modernes), Paris, 1948.

Divers Jeux rustiques, ed. V.L. Saulnier (Textes littéraires français), Paris,
Genève, 1965.

Lettres: see Y. Bellenger, *Du Bellay: Ses 'Regrets' qu'il fit dans Rome*,
Paris, 1975, pp. 416–440.

L'Olive, ed. E. Caldarini (Textes littéraires français), Genève, 1974.

*La Monomachie de David et de Goliath, ensemble plusieurs autres œuvres
poetiques*, ed. E. Caldarini (Textes littéraires français), Genève, 1981.

Les Regrets et autres Œuvres poëtiques suivis des *Antiquitez de Rome
plus un Songe*, ed. J. Joliffe, M.A. Screech (Textes littéraires français),
Genève, 1966.

General studies on Du Bellay:

C. BÉNÉ, 'Bible et inspiration religieuse chez Du Bellay', in G. Ces-
bron, *ed., Du Bellay: Actes du Colloque international d'Angers*, Angers,
1990, pp. 171–187.

H. CHAMARD, *Joachim Du Bellay, 1522–1560*, Lille, 1900 (reprint,
Genève, 1969).

Geneviève DEMERSON, 'Les obsessions linguistiques de Joachim
Du Bellay', *Acta conventus neo-latini Turonensis*, ed. J.-C. Margolin,
Paris, 1980, pp. 513–527.

Geneviève DEMERSON, 'Joachim Du Bellay et ses deux muses' [on the
article by Lloyd-Jones: see below], *Bulletin de l'Association d'Étude
sur l'Humanisme, la Réforme et la Renaissance*, VII, 1981, pp. 35–40.

Guy DEMERSON, *La mythologie classique dans l'œuvre de la Pléiade*,
Genève, 1972.

G. DICKINSON, *Du Bellay in Rome*, Leiden, 1960.

D. HARTLEY, *Patriotism in the work of Joachim Du Bellay*, Lewiston etc.,
1993.

K. LLOYD-JONES, 'L'originalité de la vision romaine chez Du Bellay', *Bulletin de l'Association d'Étude sur l'Humanisme, la Réforme et la Renaissance*, Montpellier, VI, 1980, pp. 13–21.

I.D. McFARLANE, 'Les réseaux d'images dans l'œuvre de Joachim Du Bellay', in *Textes et intertextes: Etudes sur le XVIe siècle pour Alfred Glauser*, ed. F. Gray, M. Tetel, Paris, 1979, pp. 123–146.

V.L. SAULNIER, *Du Bellay, l'homme et l'œuvre*, Paris, 1951.

M.C. SMITH, 'Joachim Du Bellay's renown as a Latin poet', *Acta Conventus neo-latini Amstelodamiensis*, ed. P. Tuynman, G.C. Kuiper and E. Kessler, München, 1979, pp. 928–942.

M.B. WELLS, *Du Bellay, a bibliography*, London, 1974.

Studies on Rome:

R. COOPER, 'Poetry in ruins: the literary context of Du Bellay's cycles on Rome', *Renaissance Studies*, III, 1989, pp. 156–166.

C. GARAUD, 'Remarques sur le thème des ruines dans la littérature chrétienne', *Phenix*, XX, 1966, pp. 148–158.

A. GRAF, *Roma nella memoria e nelle imaginazioni del medio evo*, Torino, 1915.

W.S. HECKSCHER, *Die Romruinen, Die geistigen Voraussetzung ihrer Wertung im Mittelalter und in der Renaissance*, Würzburg, 1936.

G. MARCHI, *Il mito di Roma in Francia*, Roma, 1978.

R. MORTIER, *La poétique des ruines en France, ses origines, ses variations de la Renaissance à Victor Hugo*, Genève, 1974.

W. REHM, *Europäische Romdichtung*, München, 1960.

W. REHM, *Der Untergang Roms im abendländischen Denken*, Darmstadt, 1966 (especially VII, 'Zur Entstehung des Dekadenzbegriffs in Frankreich', pp. 82–92).

A. ROUBICHOU-STRETZ, *La vision de l'histoire dans l'œuvre de la Pléiade*, Paris, 1973.

Studies on *Les Antiquitez de Rome:*

C. BÉNÉ, 'Joachim Du Bellay devant le destin de la Rome antique', *Actes du 9e Congrès de l'Association Guillaume Budé*, Paris, 1975, II, pp. 546–555.

H. CHAMARD, *Histoire de la Pléiade*, 4v., Paris, 1939–1940, II, pp. 229–259.

F.M. CHAMBERS, 'Lucan in the *Antiquitez de Rome*', *Publications of the Modern Language Association of America*, LX, 1945, pp. 937–948.

K. COLLINS, '*Les Antiquitez de Rome:* Du Bellay crosses the Rubicon', in P.A. Ramsey, *ed., Rome in the Renaissance: the City and the Myth*, Binghamton, New York, 1982, pp. 293–300.

R. DERCHE, 'Explication de texte: J. Du Bellay: *Les Antiquitez de Rome, III'*, *Information littéraire*, XXV, 1973, pp. 232–238.

M.-M. FONTAINE, 'Le système des *Antiquitez* de Du Bellay: L'alternance entre décasyllabes et alexandrins dans un recueil de sonnets', *Le sonnet à la Renaissance des origines au XVIe siècle*, Paris, 1986, pp. 67–81.

G. GADOFFRE, 'Histoire et destin dans les *Antiquitez de Rome'*, in his *Du Bellay et le sacré*, Paris, 1978, pp. 85–116.

A.L. GORDON, 'Styles of absence and presence: the *Antiquitez* and *Regrets'*, in C.M. Grisé and C.D.E. Tolton, *eds., Crossroads and perspectives: French literature of the Renaissance*, Genève, 1986, pp. 21–30.

M. HEATH, '*Les Antiquitez de Rome X–XII'*, *French Studies Bulletin*, 28, 1988, pp. 16–17.

R.A. KATZ, *The ordered text: the sonnet sequences of Du Bellay*, New York, etc., 1985.

P. DE LAJARTE, 'Formes et significations dans les *Antiquitez de Rome* de Du Bellay', in P.G. Castex *et al., Mélanges sur la littérature de la Renaissance à la mémoire de V.L. Saulnier*, Genève, 1984, pp. 727–734.

K. LLOYD-JONES, 'Du Bellay's journey from *Roma vetus* to *La Rome neufve'*, in P.A. Ramsey, *ed., Rome in the Renaissance: the City and the Myth*, Binghamton, New York, 1982, pp. 301–319.

E. MACPHAIL, 'The Roman tomb or the image of the tomb in Du Bellay's *Antiquitez'*, *Bibliothèque d'Humanisme et Renaissance*, XLVIII, 1986, pp. 359–372.

E. MACPHAIL, *The Voyage to Rome in French Renaissance literature* (Stanford French and Italian Studies, 68), Saratoga, CA., 1990.

G.W. PIGMAN III, 'Du Bellay's ambivalence towards Rome in the *Antiquitez'*, in P.A. Ramsey, *ed., Rome in the Renaissance: the City and the Myth*, Binghamton, New York, 1982, pp. 321–332.

M. QUAINTON, '*Morte peinture* and *peinture vivante* in *Les Antiquitez de Rome* and *Les Regrets'*, *Renaissance Studies*, III, 1989, pp. 167–177.

W.A. REBHORN, 'Du Bellay's imperial mistress: *Les Antiquitez de Rome* as petrarchist sonnet sequence', *Renaissance Quarterly*, XXXIII, 1980, pp. 609–622.

D. RUSSELL, 'Du Bellay's emblematic vision of Rome', *Yale French Studies*, 47, 1972, pp. 98–109.

V.L. SAULNIER, 'Commentaires sur les *Antiquitez de Rome'*, *Bibliothèque d'Humanisme et Renaissance*, XII, 1950, pp. 114–143.

M.C. SMITH, 'Looking for Rome in Rome: Janus Vitalis and his disciples' [on the *fortuna* of *Antiquitez*, III], *Revue de Littérature comparée*, 51, 1977, pp. 510–527.

M.C. SMITH, 'Janus Vitalis revisited', *Revue de Littérature comparée*, 63, 1989, pp. 69–75.

G.H. TUCKER, 'Sur les *Elogia* (1553) de Janus Vitalis et les *Antiquitez de Rome* de Joachim Du Bellay', *Bibliothèque d'Humanisme et Renaissance*, XLVII, 1985, pp. 103–112.

G.H. TUCKER, *The poet's Odyssey: Joachim Du Bellay and the* Antiquitez de Rome, Oxford, 1990.

J. VIANEY, '*Les Antiquitez de Rome*, leurs sources latines et italiennes', *Bulletin italien* (Faculté des lettres de Bordeaux, *Annales*, 4e série), I, 1901, pp. 187–199.

Studies on the *Songe*:

S. BOKDAM-HUOT, 'La forme du «songe» dans la poésie religieuse au seizième siècle', in F. Charpentier, *ed.*, *Le Songe à la Renaissance*, Saint-Étienne, 1990, pp. 137–149.

G. DEMERSON, 'Le Songe de J. Du Bellay et le sens des recueils romains' in F. Charpentier, *ed.*, *Le Songe à la Renaissance*, Saint-Étienne, 1990, pp. 169–178.

G. GADOFFRE, 'Le message codé du *Songe'*, in his *Du Bellay et le sacré*, Paris, 1978, pp. 151–182.

H. INGMAN, 'Du Bellay and the language of alchemy: the *Songe'*, *Modern Language Review*, LXXXII, 1987, pp. 844–853.

S.M. POLINER, 'Du Bellay's *Songe:* strategies of deceit, poetics of vision', *Bibliothèque d'Humanisme et Renaissance*, XLIII, 1981, pp. 509–525.

M.B. WELLS, 'Du Bellay's sonnet sequence *Songe*', *French Studies*, XXVI, 1972, pp. 1–8.

Studies on Jan van der Noot:

M. BATH, 'Verse form and pictorial space in Van der Noot's *Theatre for Worldlings*', in K.J. Höltgen *et al.*, eds., *Word and visual image: studies in the interaction of English literature and the visual arts*, Erlangen, 1988, pp. 73–105.

P. BRACHIN, 'Un disciple de Ronsard, J. van der Noot, patrice d'Anvers', *Archives des Lettres Modernes*, III, 24, 1959, 35p.

J.A. VAN DORSTEN, 'Noot, Jan van der', in *The Spenser encyclopedia* (see below, 'Hamilton'), pp. 511–512.

L. FORSTER, *Janus Gruter's English years: studies in the continuity of Dutch literature in Elizabethan England*, Leiden, 1967 (pp. 49–59 on Van der Noot in England).

L. FORSTER, 'The translator of the *Theatre for Worldlings*', *English Studies*, 48, 1967, pp. 27–34.

L. FORSTER, 'Jan van der Noot und die deutsche Renaissancelyrik: Stand und Aufgaben der Forschung', in R. Grimm & C. Wiedemann, eds., *Literatur und Geistesgeschichte: Festgabe für H.O. Burger*, Berlin, 1968.

L.S. FRIEDLAND, 'The illustrations in *The Theatre for Worldlings*', *The Huntington Library Quarterly*, 19, 1956, pp. 107–120.

R. GALLAND, 'Un poète errant de la Renaissance: Jean van der Noot et l'Angleterre', *Revue de Littérature comparée*, II, 1922, pp. 337–350.

A.J. HARPER, 'On the development of a poetic language in Northern Europe: Jan van der Noot's apocalypse sonnets and their English and German translations', *Strathclyde Modern Language Studies*, I, 1980, pp. 47–60.

A.J. HARPER, *Time and change: essays on German and European literature*, Frankfurt am Main, 1982, ch. 1, pp. 5–27.

JAN VAN DER NOOT, *A Theatre for Worldlings*, in P. Daly *et al.*, eds., *The English emblem tradition*, vol. 1, Toronto, etc., 1988.

W.J.B. PIENAAR, 'Edmund Spenser and Jonker van der Noot', *English Studies*, VIII, 1926, pp. 33–44, 67–76.

C.J. RASMUSSEN, '"Quietnesse of minde": *A Theatre for Worldlings* as a Protestant poetics', *Spenser Studies*, ed. P. Cullen and T.P. Roche, Jr., I, 1980, pp. 3–27.

Studies on Spenser and on his link with Du Bellay:

S. DORANGEON, 'Spenser traducteur de Du Bellay', in G. Cesbron, *ed., Du Bellay: Actes du Colloque international d'Angers*, Angers, 1990, pp. 497–508.

J.A. VAN DORSTEN, *The radical arts: first decade of an Elizabethan Renaissance*, Leiden, London, 1970, VII, ii, 'Spenser's *Theatre* translation', pp. 75–85.

J.A. VAN DORSTEN, 'Complaints: Ruines of Rome: by Bellay' in *The Spenser encyclopedia* (see below, 'Hamilton'), pp. 187–188.

J.A. VAN DORSTEN, 'A Theatre for Worldlings', in *The Spenser encyclopedia* (see below, 'Hamilton'), p. 685.

M.W. FERGUSON, 'Du Bellay, Joachim', in *The Spenser encyclopedia* (see below, 'Hamilton'), pp. 83–85.

M.W. FERGUSON, 'Complaints: Ruines of Rome: by Bellay', in *The Spenser encyclopedia* (see below, 'Hamilton'), pp. 185–186.

J. FUZIER, 'Spenser, traducteur du *Songe* de Du Bellay', *Bulletin de l'Association d'Étude sur l'Humanisme, la Réforme et la Renaissance*, VIII, 1982, pp. 96–101.

A.C. HAMILTON, *et al., eds., The Spenser encyclopedia*, Toronto, Buffalo, London, 1990.

A.K. HIEATT, 'The genesis of Shakespeare's *Sonnets*: Spenser's *Ruines of Rome: by Bellay*', *Publications of the Modern Language Association of America*, XCVIII, 1983, pp. 800–814.

J.M. KING, *Spenser's poetry and the Reformation tradition*, Princeton U. P., 1990.

L. MANLEY, 'Spenser and the city: the minor poems', *Modern Language Quarterly*, 43, 1982, pp. 203–227.

A.L. PRESCOTT, *French poets and the English Renaissance: studies in fame and transformation*, New Haven, 1978, pp. 46–52.

A.L. PRESCOTT, 'French Renaissance literature', in *The Spenser ency-lopedia* (see above, 'Hamilton'), pp. 320–321.

EDMUND SPENSER, *Shorter poems*, ed. W.A. Oram *et al.*, New Haven and London, 1989 [the *Ruines of Rome* and *Visions of Bellay* edited by R. Schell].

The Spenser encylopedia: see above, 'Hamilton'.

H. STEIN, *Studies in Spenser's* Complaints, New York, 1934.